THINK LIKE A
CHAMPION

THINK LIKE A
CHAMPION

*An Informal Education
In Business and Life*

DONALD J. TRUMP

with MEREDITH MCIVER

DA CAPO PRESS
A Member of the Perseus Books Group

Cataloging-in-Publication data for this book is available from the Library of Congress.

First Vanguard Press edition 2009
First Da Capo Press paperback edition 2013

ISBN 978-1-59315-530-8 (hardcover)
ISBN 978-1-59315-571-1 (paperback)
ISBN 978-0-7867-4757-3 (e-book)

Published by Da Capo Press
A Member of the Perseus Books Group
www.dacapopress.com

Da Capo Press books are available at special discounts for bulk purchases in the U.S. by corporations, institutions, and other organizations. For more information, please contact the Special Markets Department at the Perseus Books Group, 2300 Chestnut Street, Suite 200, Philadelphia, PA 19103, or call (800) 810-4145, ext. 5000, or e-mail special.markets@perseusbooks.com.

10 9 8 7

To my parents,
Mary and Fred Trump

CONTENTS

CONTENTS

CONTENTS

FOREWORD

by Robert Kiyosaki

One of the benefits of working with Donald is observing him in action in real life. Over the years, I have gotten to know the real Donald, as well as the "celebrity Donald." I have found he is the same person . . . In fact he is actually bigger in real life than his celebrity.

Working with him, I have observed him thinking, then listened to his thoughts become words and his thoughts and words become actions. In most instances, his thoughts, words, and actions are the same. Maybe this is why he is direct and blunt. He can be blunt because his thoughts, words, and actions are integrated, congruent, operating as one.

Many of us know people who are, actually, three people. They think one thing, say something else, and do not do what they say *or* think. I have observed these kinds of people, who are really three people, achieve limited success and live conflicted lives.

In early 1980, I lost my first major business. Losing everything was as horrible as you might expect. Losing everything gave power to the loser in me. Worst of all, I had lost confidence in myself. I knew what I had to do, but for some reason I simply did not do what I knew I had to do. My personal battle between 1980 and 1990 was to gain power over my own thoughts. To regain power over my thoughts, I began reading and listening to great thoughts from great people . . . and then made those thoughts mine. Slowly but surely, my business life began to turn and I began to win again.

In 1987, just after the stock market crashed, I came across Donald's book *The Art of the Deal*. My wife Kim and I put aside everything we were doing and read that book. As the world was crashing down, we had the opportunity and benefit—through Donald's thoughts, words, and actions—to see the world of business. By 1994, Kim and I were financially free. In our quiet moments, Kim and I often discuss how Donald's book inspired us to go on, even though the world was crashing down around us.

In 1997, reading his book *The Art of the Comeback* verified for us that we were following the thoughts of a great man. Very few people will talk publicly, much less write, about their mistakes, their lessons, and their comeback.

In 2004, Kim and I met Donald for the first time. Obviously he did not know who we were, yet he was extremely gracious and we thanked him for sharing his thoughts through his books.

In late 2006, Donald and I published our book, *Why We Want You To Be Rich: Two Men, One Message*. Fueled by our shared concern for people and our desire to teach, Donald and I collaborated on this book, predicting much of the financial chaos 2008 would bring.

It is an honor to write this Foreword for his book, *Think Like a Champion*, because teaching me to think like a champion is the gift Donald has given my wife and me . . . a gift he shares with the world . . . a gift more valuable than money.

ACKNOWLEDGMENTS

I would like to thank my chief assistant, Rhona Graff, for her dedication and focus throughout the process of putting this book together, and to my co-author Meredith McIver for her thoughtful work.

Working with the Vanguard Press team has been a great experience, and I'd especially like to thank Roger Cooper, Vice President and Publisher, Georgina Levitt, Associate Publisher, and Amanda Ferber, Publishing Manager, for their enthusiasm and very professional work. To Janet Saines of The Perseus Books Group, a special thank you.

INTRODUCTION

O ver the years, I have watched many people aspire to success. I am one of them, and while I haven't peaked yet, I've had a good share of success already. So I'm often asked what my "secrets" to success are. I don't think they're secrets, but every one of us needs to have a formula that works for him or her personally.

This collection of writing is an indication of the thought process that I believe can lead people to success. It has worked for me. It's another side to my personality—the more reflective side that reveals my sources and how I apply them to the big picture that is life. The persona you so often see via the world media is someone who is outgoing, confident, sometimes brash—but honest. One reason people like me is because I'm blunt. One reason people don't like me is because I'm blunt. But one reason I'm successful is that I can cut through nonsense quickly and get to the core of things.

Think Like a Champion is an example of that approach to life and business. I take a topic, think about it, dissect it, and put it back into a formula that becomes what I believe is solid advice. I have always relished putting time and energy into digging below the surface of a problem and coming up with a unique and effective answer.

While I was in school, my father, Fred C. Trump, would send inspirational quotes to me every week. Many of them were about leadership, how to be a champion in life. I learned a lot from them and I still refer to them, so they are included here for you.

I was fortunate to have a mentor in my life like my father, and I hope these writings will prove to be helpful to you. I would like to dedicate this book to the memory of my father and all that he taught me. I would hope that sharing these thoughts with you will provide you with guidance as well as inspiration.

—*Donald J. Trump*

THINK LIKE A
CHAMPION

The future belongs to those who believe
in the beauty of their dreams.

—Eleanor Roosevelt

Barack Obama
Election Ushers in
a Different World

After the election in November of 2008, I was interviewed by
Dominic Carter of New York 1 (who has recently, as of late
2009, gone through a great deal with spousal abuse) on his program called "Inside City Hall." New York 1 is an all-news program
that is popular in New York City, and Dominic has a dynamic
television presence. He describes me as "a man not known for
keeping his opinions to himself," and we covered some interesting topics.

Dominic asked about the election and I was honest about it.
McCain was in an almost impossible situation. Bush had been so
incompetent that any Republican would have a hard time unless
they could bring back Eisenhower. Bush was a disaster for the
country as well as for the Republican Party.

Then he asked me about Barack Obama. I told him that
Barack will need to be a great president because we're in serious

trouble as a country. It hasn't been this way since 1929. So he doesn't have much choice—he will simply *have* to be great, which he has a very good chance of being.

What he has done is amazing. The fact that he accomplished what he has—in one year and against great odds—is truly phenomenal. If someone had asked me if a black man or woman could become president, I would have said yes, but not yet. Barack Obama proved that determination combined with opportunity and intelligence can make things happen—and in an exceptional way.

He is not walking into an easy or enviable situation. As of October of 2008, the U.S. government reported a $237 billion deficit. The good news is that Obama seems to be well aware of the situation. His comments have led me to believe that he understands how the economy works on a comprehensive level. He has also surrounded himself with very competent people, and that's the mark of a strong leader. I have confidence he will do his best, and we have someone who is serious about resolving the problems we have and will be facing in the future. To me that is very good news.

After 9/11, this country received a lot of compassion from countries and people around the world. Within a short amount of time, however, we were hated. How did that happen? We had no dialogue with other countries because they just plain hated us. What's different today is that we have a new chance, a new beginning. The world is excited about Barack Obama and the new United States. Let's keep it that way.

Whatever games are played with us,
we must play no games with ourselves.

—Ralph Waldo Emerson

~⌒⌐

Essays, Assets, and
Stephen King

In the *New York Times Book Review* of September 30, 2007, is an essay by Stephen King on the short story. As you most likely know, Stephen King is the prolific and very successful author of sixty books and nearly 400 short stories. One of his short stories won the O. Henry Prize in 1996. His point in his essay is that in reviewing the state of the short story today, he notes that they seem to "feel show-offy, and written for editors and teachers, rather than for readers." This is an insightful comment and it got me to thinking about why we write and who we think our audience might be.

I like essays and so I can relate to the short story, although the short story is a fictional prose tale. The short story is not an easy medium, as any writer will tell you, because you must be concise. Essays are a bit the same, because they are succinct and specific. If you read Stephen King's essay, you will see that he gets his point across beautifully in the span of one page.

3

I may not be Stephen King, but I can appreciate what he does. You may not be a mogul yet, but I think you can appreciate the complexities of what I have to deal with daily. Stephen King is pointing out that the market for short stories is limited these days, so the writers of short stories seem more determined than ever to make their mark—but on the editors who might be able to get their story into print, not the reader, who might be expecting to be entertained. A valid consideration, I will say. We all have target markets and the demographics are important, no matter what your industry may be.

In short, Stephen King is astutely acknowledging that the short story writers of today are protecting their assets by targeting their writing to the people who will most likely be able to get it into print. Their second consideration is the reader because, unless they consider the editor first, their reader will have no chance of ever seeing the short story, no matter how wonderful or how mediocre it might be. It's an intelligent approach, but I can understand the point Mr. King is making when he laments the fact that the stories seem prefabricated to appeal to a certain audience—editors and teachers, in this case.

When I build a residential building, for example, I will first consider who will be living there. I study the demographics, as does any business person, whether you're in advertising or residential property management. To get the message out, I will also have to appeal to the people who will choose—or not choose—to promote the building. By now, my name is big enough and equated with the gold standard to the extent that I don't have to say too much about it. The name Trump is a guarantee of a certain level of quality. Stephen King mentions that short stories seem to be delegated to the bottom shelf at the bookstores. He says the American short story is alive but not well these days. The main reason seems to be that the target market is simply dwindling.

I think that he does a spot-on analysis of the situation when he notices that the stories seem to be written for publication purposes, not for the edification of the reader. I know that if I did something that was intended to impress the so-called critics that I would be selling not only myself short, but other people as well. That's one reason I'm liked as well as disliked. In fact, one critic from the *New York Times*, Herbert Muschamp, mentioned that I do better when I choose to ignore my critics than when I pay attention to them. I have to agree, and Stephen King might agree to that as well when it comes to the fate of the short story.

Being true to yourself and your work is an asset. Remember that assets are worth protecting. No one will ever tell you it will be easy to stick to your own convictions, but I believe it is necessary. Otherwise, what are you doing and who are you doing it for? Keep it straight and simple. You will be richer—in more ways than one—in the long run.

There is one thing stronger than all the armies of the world,
and that is an idea whose time has come.

—Victor Hugo

~~~

Innovation

People often talk about something new being "innovative."
Most of the time, it's simply putting together existing elements
to create what appears to be new. I was touted as being innovative
when I came up with the mixed-use condominium and hotel
tower, which I did with the Trump International Hotel & Tower
in New York City. Since then, the concept has been copied (by
myself and others) and it has proven to be tremendously successful, nationally and internationally.

To me, the idea was common sense, and I didn't think I was
being particularly creative. When I look back, maybe I was. But
when I read subsequent articles about innovation and certain in-
ventors, it got me thinking about how one might become an
innovator, which is something I think is important for students to
think about.

I remember reading about a composer named Steve Reich
who came up with a new idea called phasing, which is like windshield wipers going in and out of synch. Apparently he was caught
in a traffic jam one rainy day and the rhythm of the windshield

wipers caught his attention and he applied what he heard to his musical compositions. He has had a significant influence on contemporary music, and I think he's a great example as an innovator. Sometimes new ideas can come from something as mundane and functional as your windshield wipers. The key is to pay attention and keep your brain and senses open to new stimuli.

It also helps to be thinking of two things at once—multilevel focusing is what I call it. The intersecting of ideas is when innovation will follow—thinking in musical terms while listening to your windshield wipers, or thinking of a hotel tower and condominiums at one time, or maybe watching a stone roll and imagining a wheel. Who knows what will result? Sometimes it will be fantastic and other times it won't, but it gets the mind working in new dimensions that can sometimes prove fruitful.

This can also happen without deliberately attempting to be innovative, so the other technique to employ—consciously and unconsciously—is to keep an open mind. That's very important in business as well as in the creative arts. Don't limit yourself to staid thinking because you want to excel in business. My first book was called *The Art of the Deal* because I view business deals as being an art form. Maybe that's why I've been a successful dealmaker. I employ both sides of my brain when I'm thinking and working.

You may be aware of the number phi (pronounced "fee"), which has an astonishing history. It's been employed by people from Pythagoras to da Vinci, and most likely the builders of the pyramids used it as well. It's been around for a long time and the number itself is 1.6180339887. It's called the golden ratio, and if you want to know more specifics, you can read *The Golden Ratio* by Mario Livio, who goes into great detail about it. My point is that it appears that some people use the number deliberately, and other people know it subconsciously and it can appear in their work with or without intention. But it can be used intentionally, and very often is. It's very mysterious, as this ratio appears in un-related works and natural phenomena, from the chambered nau-tilus to galaxies to artwork and architecture. It can make your innovative attempts a little easier when you make an effort to un-derstand that there are mysteries in life and to be open to them.

I'm not advising you to dwell on the mysterious—a success-ful life requires common sense and hard work—but to be aware of things that are sometimes inexplicable because they can be a big step toward innovation. We don't really create, but we assem-ble what has been created for us. Be a great assembler—no mat-ter what your interests may be—and you'll be on your way to inventiveness. A big mind requires a variety of thoughts and im-pulses to keep it well occupied, so make sure you keep your mind engaged in the best ways possible. It could very well be your call-ing card for success.

*Coming together is a beginning, keeping together
is progress, working together is success.*

—Henry Ford

The Importance
of Being
a Team Player

I have always known the importance of having the ability to be a team player, even though I am an entrepreneur. In a big sense, we're all in this together, and thinking otherwise won't give us the results we might be aiming for. More than ever, working together is integral to survival as well as to success.

As I was thinking of this, I remembered a couple of good examples of team players. Most of us know of Tom Brokaw, the television journalist and author. He has received many awards and is highly esteemed within his industry as well as with the public. I remember when *The Apprentice* first premiered and it was doing very well—it was the number one rated show that week and I had been invited to sit in George Steinbrenner's box for a Yankees game. Tom was there with his lovely wife, and he tapped me on the shoulder and said, "Thanks, Donald, for what you've done for NBC. We really appreciate it."

What he said was a perfect example of team spirit. We were on the same network, and he cared about what I'd done for them. "Them" became "us," and I understood where he was coming from immediately. He may be famous, but he knows his programs aren't just about him. My program isn't just about me, either. In fact, as you will discover as you gain wisdom over the years, most of the things you do will rarely be just about you. Tom cared about the network, and his team was being helped by the success of *The Apprentice*. His comment gave me great insight into his integrity as a person—and maybe that's why everyone at NBC, as well as the public, loves and respects him.

Likewise, while I was standing backstage in Los Angeles for the Emmy Awards when *The Apprentice* had been nominated for an award, Debra Messing, who had won acclaim and an Emmy Award for her performance in *Will and Grace*, was standing nearby. I had always liked Debra, maybe because her hair is so great, but she came up to me and very graciously thanked me for the success of *The Apprentice*. Once again I realized that here was another team player of note—her show was also on NBC.

It's been a few years, but I can clearly recall the day Jeff Zucker came to my office to ask me if I'd host *Saturday Night Live*. One reason I wanted to say yes to Jeff was that *Saturday Night Live* was an NBC show and I was a part of their team. Team spirit was important, and I have to say it was a great choice. Everyone had a good time, and everyone won.

My point is that keeping the team spirit alive and well in your personal and professional lives will give you some very good, even surprising, results. Plus, it's a great feeling to take the high road. Never negate the power of the team, and you'll be a team player of note as well as power.

*At times our own light goes out and is rekindled by
a spark from another person. Each of us has cause to
think with deep gratitude of those who have
lighted the flame within us.*

—Albert Schweitzer

~❧~

An Early
Thanksgiving

O n the day before the Rosh Hashanah holiday each year for
the past eighteen years, I receive a message from a Rabbi in
Los Angeles. I am not Jewish, but have many observant Jews who
work for me, so I am well aware of the holiday schedule and that
Rosh Hashanah is their New Year, a time for celebration.

I find his message of thanks to be especially resonant because
he and his wife lost their son years ago, yet they call to remind
themselves (and me) of the many blessings they've had in life. The
reason the Rabbi calls me every year is a wonderful example of
the spirit of thanksgiving: Back in 1988, he and his wife had a
three-year-old son who had an illness that was confounding the
doctors in Los Angeles. One day the boy's father called me to see
if they could borrow my jet. He didn't know me, and I didn't
know him. But he explained that no commercial airline would fly

his son due to the extensive equipment required to sustain his life. It was considered too big of a risk. I had small children at the time, and I immediately said yes to his request. How could I say no?

I sent my jet out and brought the little boy and his parents to New York with the hope that doctors here might find a cure for the severe breathing illness from which he was suffering. His cure was not to be, but his parents have remained grateful to this day. I am always touched that they remember me.

In these recent days of upheaval in our country, I found the Rabbi's yearly message to be an insight into a good way to handle difficult and even tragic times—to find a blessing in the midst of adversity. This family and their faith is a wonderful example for all of us, and I would like to thank them for their yearly reminder. We should realize that we all have a lot to be thankful for, whether it's New Year's, Thanksgiving, or just another Wednesday in our lives.

The beginning of every government starts
with the education of our youth.

—PYTHAGORAS

~~⁀

Learning Is a
New Beginning

Pythagoras interpreted the universe through numbers. As a businessman, that always appealed to me. It makes sense. He was
a philosopher and a mathematician, and he knew the importance
of learning. Pythagoras lived a long time ago, but a lot of things
have remained the same, like the significance of education for both
individuals and society.

Whenever I start something new, I know I have a lot to learn.
This does not discourage me—in fact it gives me energy. It is similar to the feeling of a new beginning, a fresh start. When I started
building golf courses, I had a tremendous amount to learn, but it
was fantastic to be doing something brand new and I loved learning the details of golf course design. If someone had told me thirty
years ago I'd be developing golf courses, I would have thought
they were joking. But it's something I've truly enjoyed doing.

It's important to remain open to new ideas and new information. Being a know-it-all is like shutting the door to great

discoveries and opportunities. Keep your door open every day to something new and energizing. Sometimes I wonder what will show up, which is a terrific way to start every day. Other times I might have to search a bit on my own, which is why books and educational tools can be wonderful and should be readily available. Maybe I'm just fortunate, but I'm never bored. In fact, I think that's a big reason behind my success.

Once in awhile—or often is even better—ask yourself this question: What do I need to know more about? Maybe it's world history. With the events of today being what they are, it's probably a good idea to know a little about how different cultures have evolved and are operating. Maybe it's something else. I make an effort to read newspapers with ample international coverage and the *Financial Times* on a daily basis because it's important to my business to know what's going on worldwide. That alone can require serious attention every day. For you it may be something else.

These days, we don't have many excuses for having a blind spot. We all have access to information with relatively little effort, and, back to the ancient Greeks, Socrates is famed for having said, "There is only one thing I know, and that is I know nothing." Pretty tough words coming from an esteemed scholar and philosopher, but it opened him up to more knowledge every day. In other words, start every day with a clean slate. Give yourself a new beginning by opening up your mind.

If I'd started in business thinking I knew everything, I'd have been sunk before I got started. Don't make that mistake. There are a lot of hidden aspects in every industry, and you will find out how complex seemingly simple things can be. For example, to get a building built in New York City requires knowledge of zoning, contractors, architects, air rights, tax laws, unions, and about a thousand other things. I had a lot to learn and no one else could learn it for me. But every day I would learn something, apply it, and make progress. Believe me, being a developer didn't happen overnight.

Never think of learning as being a burden or studying as being boring. It may require some discipline, but it can be an adventure. It can also prepare you for a new beginning. Notice the first word in my *Think Big* credo: Think. That's the first step. Use everything in your power to utilize and develop that capability, and you'll be in for some great surprises.

A leader has the right to be beaten,
but never the right to be surprised.

—NAPOLEON BONAPARTE

Learn to Think
on Your Feet

I've already spoken about complacency and how it can ruin your chances for success. It's the same as being in a rut and deciding to stay there. That's why I like to advise people to live on the edge—it's the opposite of complacency, and the same as thinking on your feet.

Ever notice how your senses are heightened when you are in challenging situations? It's like having an adrenalin rush that gives you extra energy. If you see every day as a challenge, you'd be surprised how efficient you can become and how much can be accomplished. People often say they "hit the street running," which is another way of saying they did their prep work and were ready.

One of the most obvious lessons on *The Apprentice* is for the candidates to learn to think quickly. They are under a time constraint to finish their assignments, and as we've noticed, it's important that they have a Plan B in line. If Plan A doesn't work, they're prepared for it and they won't lose much time. They are learning to think ahead, to be prepared, and to cover their bases. These are basic ingredients for success in business.

When I started out in business, I spent a great deal of time researching every detail that might be pertinent to the deal I was interested in making, and I still do the same today. People often comment on how quickly I operate, which is true. But the reason I can move quickly is that I've done the background work first, which often no one sees. Just because you don't see someone working doesn't mean they haven't been working in their spare or private time. I prepare myself thoroughly, and then when it is time to move ahead, I am ready to sprint.

Being able to think on your feet is the result of training and discipline. You can't sprint unless you have built up the strength to do so. Building the stamina is up to you. If you don't work at it, it's not going to happen by wishful thinking. You have to dedicate yourself to it every day. In other words, set a goal and work toward it. Athletes know that no one else can do the training for them, and business people should have the same discipline. You have to be self-reliant.

Have you ever said to yourself, "I wish I'd thought of that!"? I've heard people say that when they come across something very clever or something fantastic. One way to learn to think on your feet is to ask yourself what you should be thinking of this very moment. Do it right now, and then see other people saying, "I wish I'd thought of that—what a great idea!" You'd be surprised how many good ideas you might have if you'd give yourself the opportunity to think about them. Thinking takes time. It's the preparation for being able to think on your feet. First things first: First we walk, then we run, then we sprint.

Thoreau said, "I know of no more encouraging fact than the unquestioned ability of a man to elevate his life by conscious endeavor." That is not only an encouraging statement, it is also an empowering one. It means you can accomplish a lot by applying your brainpower and then moving forward with it. Thought without action won't amount to much in the long run. Those great ideas you have will remain great ideas unless you actively do something with them.

Don't wait for dire circumstances to test your quick-thinking ability. Test yourself daily. Be on alert at all times. As Napoleon said, "A leader has the right to be beaten, but never the right to be surprised." See yourself as a leader—starting right now. It will mean you are self-reliant, responsible, and not apt to being unnecessarily surprised by the vicissitudes of life, whether you are in business or not. Being prepared cannot be overestimated, and if you want to hit the big time running, you'd better be able to think on those feet of yours.

He who can no longer pause to wonder
and stand rapt in awe, is as good as dead;
his eyes are closed.

—ALBERT EINSTEIN

~~~)

Strive for Wholeness

Ever hear the saying "Get the big picture"? It amazes me when people can leave out or ignore big pieces in a picture or pretend nothing is missing. It's like ordering a pizza and getting a pie with a few slices already removed—and still thinking it's a whole pie. Wouldn't you wonder where those pieces went?

I've encountered people who don't wonder about anything. Sometimes I wonder if they are in shock or something. Maybe they're just afraid to strive for the big picture or the whole pie, or maybe they don't think they're worth the whole pie. Whatever it is, don't let yourself fall into any of those categories. Don't ever sell yourself short. That's bad business on every level, even the metaphysical.

If striving for wholeness means diminishing your competition, then your competition wasn't much to begin with. A lot of life is about survival of the fittest and adaptation, as Darwin pointed out. It's not all there is, but it's an indication of how the world has evolved in historical terms. We've seen many empires come and go—the Roman Empire, the Ottoman Empire, and so forth. There have always been surges of power. Sometimes they last for centuries. Even so, some of us have never heard of them as of today. In other words, things change. We have to keep up with the changes and move forward or we will be holding some moldy pieces of the pie.

As The Trump Organization has moved forward, I have very much seen it as a living organism that needs to be fed and replenished. It needs to be whole, which requires many sections fitting together and working together tightly. It is a daily requirement on my part to make sure all the ingredients are there and working together to make the best product possible. I can't have any missing pieces. I can't have any ingredients that aren't the best. Those are my standards, and it's my responsibility to make sure they are kept.

See yourself as an organization. Pay attention to every facet of your life. What's strong? What's weak? What's missing? What can you do to make the big picture better? Whatever you do, don't stagnate. Don't become complacent. Don't pretend that 50 percent is enough, whether you're giving or receiving. Things move too quickly today to fall into that trap.

When I realized how fast the world moves, I decided to double up on my work hours. That wasn't a big sacrifice because I love what I'm doing and I've always been a hard worker. I'm happier and more productive now than I ever was. But I kept the pace in order to keep up with my environment, which is a fast one. New York is known for being fast. You can adapt or lose out. I chose to adapt. Make your choices accordingly. People who want to compete with me will have to keep up with me.

I had a dynamic, very well-qualified, very well-educated young man come to work for me. I remember thinking, this guy is going to be great. Was I ever wrong. He took so long to explain anything that every time I saw him, I began to dread any kind of interaction with him. He was just too slow. He was thorough and painstaking, but he couldn't keep up with the required pace. He couldn't adapt to his environment, and despite his qualifications, he was unable to get the big picture and figure out how to fit in. It was a happy day for me when he departed. Don't let that happen to you. Learn to adapt. Learn to keep learning.

Very few of us are completed projects. It's an ongoing process. Even being a prodigy, Mozart worked at what he did. We have to assemble the bits and pieces constantly in order to achieve the whole. But we have to assemble creatively and passionately to get anywhere near the whole. It's another way of covering your bases for the most effective game. Strive for wholeness and keep your sense of wonder intact, and you will find yourself ready for a grand slam.

An achievement is a bondage.
It obliges one to a higher achievement.

—Albert Camus

Give Your
Higher Self
a Chance

When the achiever achieves, it's not a plateau, it's a beginning. Achievers move forward at all times—they have anticipation for their next deal and have another goal immediately lined up. It's enthusiasm that can't be fabricated—it's either there, or it's not. Achievers go for the challenge, so the next deal is what they're thinking about. They have an obligation to themselves to best themselves. That's living in the highest realm.

Your higher self is in direct opposition to your comfort zone. An indication of life is growth, and signs of growth have to be there. You've heard people refer to a city as vibrant, and what that means is that it's growing and it's lively—it is not stagnating. See yourself as a city if you must, with all the inner and outer workings necessary to keep yourself thriving and efficient.

There are so many "fine lines" in life that when people say life is an art, they're not too far off. I've said before that I see my work as an art form, and that's one reason why. We all know that fine line between something great and something extraordinary. Sometimes it's almost imperceptible, or impossible to define. What makes da Vinci's *Mona Lisa* so exceptional? There are millions of different answers, but it mesmerizes people. It's mysterious and brings us to another realm, a different dimension.

Our higher selves can serve to transport us to becoming visionaries. The word visionary evokes a lot of images and definitions, some even being a "castle-builder" or a Don Quixote. It often connotes someone who is idealistic. There is nothing wrong with that as long as it's contained within reason. Visionaries move the world along into new dimensions. Look at Bill Gates, for example, in technology; or Mark Burnett in reality TV; or Pablo Picasso, Stravinksy, and other greats of the twentieth century. They were groundbreakers who followed their own instincts and led us in new directions.

Our higher self will often lead us into new waters, and for a good reason. No one wants to spend their life treading water just to keep from going under. That is futile and disheartening. Sometimes we do things to build up experience and stamina to prepare us, but it's to prepare us for something bigger. Always know you could be on the precipice of something great—that's being connected to your higher self. It's also a good way to keep those negative thoughts far away.

Sometimes our goals aren't necessarily concrete. Sometimes it's a feeling of something great that will happen, and so we're open to it. That doesn't mean we sit around waiting for something to just happen—very often it happens while we're working away on something else. Being industrious can be a magnet for new ideas, while idleness and inertia can be magnets for negativity.

One of the worst fears we can have is the fear to attempt something. That can leave you feeling bereft for no particular reason except that maybe you will have missed your purpose. There is always the possibility of failure, but there is a greater chance of success if you actually try to do something versus doing nothing. I wasn't sure I'd be a success on the radio, but I went for it and my program on Clear Channel was a big hit. But I had to take the chance first to find out.

Life can be an adventure of the best sort if you will give your higher self a chance. We all have something unique to offer. Our work is to find out what that is and to work at it with a passion. So don't tread water. Get out there and go for it.

Experience is one thing
you can't get for nothing.

—OSCAR WILDE

~~⌐

Wisdom

I remember reading a short book that was entirely based on the question: What does wisdom mean to you? People from every profession, every walk of life, and every possible background contributed their thoughts. All these people had been successful. The answers were diverse, but I realized they tended to have a few common denominators: experience, integrity, and knowledge.

I was relatively young when I read this book, and in fact I can't remember the title of it. It was left on a table in the library at school so I just happened upon it. I understood the emphasis on knowledge, and could see the value of experience even though I hadn't had much yet, so what stood out the most to me was integrity. Very often it was combined with the value of reputation, and I think that's when my approach to a quality brand name was in gestation.

My father had already established a strong brand name in the outer boroughs of New York City as a developer, and people knew his work would have an inherent quality to it. They wouldn't have to guess or feel they were taking a chance if it had the Trump

31

name on it. That's how he built his reputation. When I went into business for myself, I made a point to establish a reputation that bankers and other professionals would be comfortable with, and I knew that eventually my integrity as a businessman would be intact. People are more apt to want to work with you if they feel they can trust you—an important consideration especially if one wants financial backing for projects.

Whether you are a full- or part-time student now is a good time to think about your future, whether it's brand new or a new beginning. Make certain things your guideposts. It's a good sign you're reading this because that means you are serious about your education and gaining knowledge. That's something that was emphasized to me as a student, and I made a greater effort to learn everything I could in order to gain wisdom.

What was pointed out—and what I fully realized later—is that wisdom comes as a result of several factors: one being experience, and one being knowledge. It's something you can't teach someone else—you have to achieve it on your own. It also has to do with insight, which comes with experience as well.

I realize now when I can assess a situation quickly that it's a result of wisdom I've gained through a variety of experiences. It's a bit like being able to trust your instincts because you've had a good record of successes. It's very hard for me to just give you this wisdom—you have to get there yourself. But these pointers were helpful to me as a student, and they are worth thinking about.

Another way to gain wisdom is to read about the greats in history and those in your specific field of interest. I learned a great deal by reading about Winston Churchill, Abraham Lincoln, and people who had been in pivotal places in world history. They had to be very equipped to deal with what they were handed. Their situations may have been a matter of fate, destiny, and timing, but they had the experience and wisdom to deal effectively with their circumstances. Imagine having many thousands or even millions of people affected by your actions and decisions, and you will have an inkling of the immense responsibility these people had. It can make our problems seem small in comparison, and it can enlarge our minds in order to comprehend a bigger picture of duty and competence.

I remember realizing back in school that two things in particular seemed to shape the world as I knew it then—war and nature. Nature is a powerful force and so is war. It changes the landscape of countries and cultures, and nature can just plain change the landscape. So I spent time studying wars and their impact on where we are today in civilization. That's a big assignment and I'm by no means an expert, but it is worth spending some time to know how and why we are where we are today.

One book that I would suggest to you, because it is valuable for business and managerial strategies, is *The Art of War* by Sun Tzu. This was apparently written in the sixth century BC and is a study of military strategy. It has been influential to leaders for many centuries, and General Douglas MacArthur studied it as well as other famed military strategists throughout history. It may sound like an unusual business school recommendation, but believe me, it isn't. It's valuable and worth your time.

By comparison, another famed book is Machiavelli's *The Prince,* which is more about political conflict and the qualities necessary for leadership than war or business, but its emphasis on power becomes a negative factor. Ethics and integrity seem to get lost somewhere in the shuffle, and therefore the word Machiavellian has become a pejorative term. It's a better use of your time to read *The Art of War.*

There are many roads to wisdom and many wonderful books to educate us on our way. I'm sure you'll discover your own favorites, but the first step is to take the time to read and learn in the first place. In the long term, this will save you time because you will be learning from people who have already been faced with serious issues and who have been victorious. Remember, you need knowledge and experience first. Wisdom will come provided you give it a chance to develop. First things first, and you will be pleased at what will follow. The achievement of wisdom will be all yours.

If you want to understand today,
you have to search yesterday.

—Pearl S. Buck

~~~

The More You Learn,
the More You Realize
What You Don't Know

Iremember when a friend was studying history and he spent a long time on World War II. I mentioned that he must be an expert after the amount of time he'd spent on it, and he replied, "It only made me realize how much I didn't know. Because in order to understand WWII, you have to go back to WWI. So now I'm studying WWI, and I'm sure I'll have to go further back to understand how WWI came about. It will be a never-ending process." This guy was a real scholar, but he mentioned that studying history had made him very humble—because he knew he'd never know it all no matter how much he studied.

I always remember what this guy said, about learning how much he didn't know, and how every time you learn one thing, it leads to another thing and so on. He went on to become a highly respected historian, but I can assure you that he isn't resting on his many laurels. The humility that studying history has given him keeps him young and eager to learn more, no matter how erudite he is considered to be. He's a great example of remaining a student— every day is another opportunity to learn something new.

Sometimes we are so zealous to become successful that we forget about what is significant. The background for success should include some intrinsic values as well as monetary values. We should be aware of our culture and other cultures, our history and their history, and we should not live in what has been termed "a cultural vacuum." Someone once said that not knowing history was like being a leaf that didn't know it was part of a tree. That's an interesting visual and it applies to many people. We are individually responsible for our education, and that applies whether you're in school or not.

If I sound tough on this subject, I am. I see no value whatsoever in believing ignorance to be an attribute. It isn't. It's good to start each day by saying to yourself, "What can I learn today that I didn't know before?" It opens you up to more information and net worth as an individual. Why live restricted lives due to lack of knowledge when there are so many resources available to us today?

Another interesting aspect of history is that it will lead us to seeing that we are all a part of it. History isn't just in the past—it's happening now. How can you know what you're a part of if you don't know what it is to begin with? The world didn't start with your birth, and it won't end with your death either. That doesn't mean you're not a part of the scheme of things. To the contrary, it means that you are.

Back to the leaf image. What if you know you are a leaf, but you're not sure what a tree is? I'd say the best thing to do is to find out what a tree is. It's pretty simple. It reminds me of an *Apprentice* task that's enough of a challenge to set the apprentices out to discover and research some things before they jump in to the task at hand.

I was listening to some Europeans once and they seemed to agree that Americans didn't seem to know their roots. Of course, their roots go back for many more centuries than ours and may be easier to decipher because many of us have ancestors from different countries. But it gave me a reason to think about what they said, and I realized in many cases they were right. I recently went to Scotland, as my mother's side of the family is of Scottish ancestry, and I've spent time studying that country and therefore my heritage. It could even explain why I love golf so much—it originated in Scotland.

I found that I enjoyed learning about Scotland and it has broadened my horizons as well as my interests as a businessman. I am building a golf course in Aberdeen, Scotland, that will be spectacular, and I very much enjoyed my visit and meeting the people from that culture and country. I also realized I still have a lot to learn, which will no doubt lead me into more interesting ventures as well as adventures.

Take my advice and never be a know-it-all. First of all, it's impossible to know everything, and second of all, it's just no fun—for you or anyone else. And third, you will be missing out on some great adventures. So remember to think big by expanding your horizons at the same time you're expanding your net worth. That's what significant success is about.

For what is the best choice, for each individual,
is the highest it is possible for him to achieve.

—ARISTOTLE

Think Like
a Champion

Champions are born and champions are made. One definition of a champion is someone who shows marked superiority. Another definition is someone who is a winner of first prize or first place in competition. We've all heard of Olympic champions, and we've probably all seen a few on television. What comes to mind when I see their amazing ability is the amount of training they have endured, the sacrifices they've made, and the courage they've had to have to get where they are. Those are some of the attributes of a champion.

They also wanted to achieve something special. Ordinary wouldn't be enough for someone who has the mindset of a champion. Champions think big. Champions work in a big-time way. Champions are focused. Champions are disciplined. Come to think of it, champions think like champions. As Jack Dempsey said, "A champion is someone who gets up when he can't." Let's hope that applies to you.

When I'm having an especially tough day, I often think it's like a race and I'd better have the endurance to get through it. Somehow the endurance will surface, because I don't want to wind up feeling beaten. Billie Jean King said, "Champions take responsibility. When the ball is coming over the net, you can be sure I want the ball." I understand what she was talking about, because I'm the same way in that respect.

I have a box at the U.S. Open every year because I love to watch those champions go at it. You can learn a lot from watching the experts, whether you're interested in sports, the arts, or whatever. One thing they all have in common is the same mindset: They want to win, they want to be the best. Not the runner-up, but the best. That's a very important thing to consider. I've seen very talented people fail because deep down I think they were afraid of winning. Winning comes with a responsibility. Champions rise to that responsibility. Search yourself carefully to make sure you're ready and capable. If you're not, do something about it. It's an important element of success.

Most of you know that I'm a golfer. I've always said that golf is a brain game, which it is, but it is a demanding sport technically and is a game of finesse. You cannot play golf halfheartedly and expect to get anywhere with your game. You have to concentrate and you have to have patience. As the legendary golfer Bobby Jones said, "It is nothing new or original to say that golf is played one stroke at a time. But it took me many years to realize it." We win in our daily lives by being careful with every day, by having a champion's view of each moment.

Let's take a look at Aristotle's quote at the beginning of this essay. That is self-scrutiny at its highest. It really is the best choice to go for the highest achievement possible. Why set your goals too low? Did you ever hear a child saying they want to be nothing when they grow up? They are full of dreams and plans, and rarely are they mediocre aspirations. They want to be presidents, doctors, astronauts, scientists, and so on. They're on the right track and have the right mindset. If you need to, bring yourself back to when you had high achievement as a goal. Not everyone can be the world champion at something, but you can strive to be the best you can be. That's the first step—and a daily responsibility.

Champions go the extra mile. We all know when we've done just enough and when we've really exerted ourselves. Make an effort to exert yourself—every day. Don't fail because you never allowed yourself to get started! Don't avoid success because you think the responsibility might be too much—just focus and get going! You'd be surprised at what intelligent effort can produce. Alexander Graham Bell said something that I always remember: "Concentrate all your thoughts upon the work at hand. The sun's rays do not burn until brought to a focus." Pay attention to these things and you will be on your way to thinking like a champion—and becoming one.

Art is a lie
which makes us see the truth.

—Pablo Picasso

~~⌒

I View My Work
as an Art Form

Picasso was not only a great artist, he was also a good business-man. He knew the value of his work and he didn't make ex-cuses for it. He told a story once about someone who visited his studio, stood in front of a painting, and asked him, "What does it represent?" Picasso's response was, "Two hundred thousand dol-lars." He was telling the truth and in no uncertain terms. Picasso obviously viewed his art as a business, which it was. I view my business as an art, which it is. You should view your work that way, too.

Here's why. Artists are known for their dedication to their ideals, to their muse—whatever that might be—and for their per-severance in getting things just right. Those are admirable traits to possess. They will go to great lengths to achieve the desired result. In 2005, a Beethoven manuscript was discovered in a library, and he made so many changes and scratches on it that there were holes punctured through the pages in some places. This work was found to be done toward the end of his life, so he wasn't a novice at writing music at that point. That's just how he worked—he was a perfectionist who wouldn't settle for less than his best. He didn't need to impress anyone—except himself. That's a good way to be, whether you're a businessperson or a musician.

Compete with yourself to be the best you can be.

That's the mindset of entrepreneurs—they know that competing with others might possibly lower their own standards. That may sound tough, but it's the truth. You have to have your own vision and stick with it. Picasso definitely had his own way of seeing things that certainly worked to his advantage, artistically and financially. Don't be afraid of being unique. It's like being afraid of your best self.

Back to Picasso's statement about art being a lie. One take on that is that the arts very often make the difficult look effortless. How hard is it to put paint on a canvas? Easy if you don't know what you're doing. A little more complex if you do know what you're doing. In my first book, *The Art of the Deal,* I chose the title for those very reasons. Anyone in business knows that negotiating and making deals requires a lot of background work. People don't see me doing that part, but it doesn't mean I don't do it. For example, when people see the beautiful marble in Trump Tower, they see that it looks fantastic, but they usually have no idea what I went through personally to achieve the end result. No one cares about the blood, sweat, and tears that art or beauty can require. It's the end result that matters.

Art is also representational. In other words, it's not life, but it's about life. It can point to truths that we might not notice in our busy daily lives. It gives us a reflection. When I do a deal, it's a reflection of my astuteness as a businessman. I strive for a comprehensive approach, much as an artist would. No matter what your field is, you can learn a lot by emulating that approach as much as possible.

My work as a builder combines both craftsmanship and art, and I refuse to settle for less. I didn't have to use a rare marble when I built Trump Tower, but it would make a difference and I knew it. So when I say I view my work as an art form, you can bet that I'm as meticulous as any artist is about their materials and the desired result. If you will do the same, I think you'll surprise yourself at how high your standards will become.

Don't sell yourself short. Life is an art, business is an art, so be an artist and best yourself.

I don't think much of a man
who is not wiser today than he was yesterday.

—Abraham Lincoln

Experience teaches only the teachable.

—Aldous Huxley

~

Building
Connected
Thoughts

Comprehensive education dissolves the line between knowing too much and knowing too little on a variety of subjects—subjects that are necessary for success. I was reminded of this recently when I interviewed a young man who was very well versed in his field of expertise and almost uneducated in every other subject that was brought up. It was like he had tunnel vision, and although I admired his knowledge of his field, I had to realize that, considering the scope of my enterprises, he might not be a great fit because of his limited interests. This gave me the idea for this article, and I think it's something all of you should consider as you are furthering your education and/or entering your careers.

Aldous Huxley, the great thinker and author of *Brave New World,* wrote an essay in 1959 titled "Integrate Education" that is still pertinent today. He emphasized the importance of building bridges in knowledge and thought, and the word he mentions for this is pontifex, or bridge-builder. It's an interesting image to keep in mind as we study and learn. By doing so, we increase our learning capacity to include and connect ideas and subjects that may not specifically pertain to our area of interest, but that may serve us well to pay attention to.

Oddly enough, as I was thinking of this situation, I was looking through the February 5, 2007, issue of *Time* magazine, which featured a letter written by Huxley in 1954, under the heading of "Classic Letter." This letter is so right on that it could be contemporary. It addresses the misinterpretations by critics and the press in their reviews, and while he admits their footnotes are "snappy," he goes onto say that, "Snappiness, alas, is apt to be in inverse ratio to accuracy." This guy knew what he was talking about on a variety of levels and subjects, and whether you agree with him or not, his ideas are well presented.

We've all heard the saying "connect the dots." I see it as having enough knowledge to be *able* to connect the dots in a reasonable and informed way. The young man I interviewed could not do this. I wasn't asking for an in-depth review of each topic presented, but an awareness of at least what the topic was. I've mentioned before the importance of keeping up with global events on a daily basis if you are planning to get anywhere in this world. Considering the availability of news, blind spots can't really be rationalized anymore, no matter where you might be living. Information is available to everyone, and if you aren't plugging into it, it will eventually work against you—maybe on your first interview. Don't learn this the hard way!

Another tactic for being your own bridge-builder is to visualize how much time is saved when you cross a bridge, versus fording a river or traversing a canyon. It's also a safeguard for falling into a gap that might take you weeks or months to get yourself out of. We are not omniscient, and sometimes things work out for a reason in a different way than we had planned, but take the time to prepare yourself for your goals. I work at that every single day. I've learned that things don't just automatically fall into line because I want them to. Be proactive in your pursuit of knowledge.

As I write this, I remind myself that if you are reading it, you are most likely someone intent on improving your intelligence quota and someone who is already motivated. So I want you to ask yourself: What is it that you are aiming for? What precisely is your motivation? What's the point of building a bridge if you're not sure you want to get to other side, or if you don't know what you'll do once you get there? A bridge must serve a specific purpose, and your goals have to be just that specific. Visualization is a powerful tool for bringing your intentions into focus.

I was having a conversation a few years ago with a few people when one guy mentioned that the Trump name had become a famous brand around the world and then added, "What's in a name?" He then sort of laughed and said to me, "in your case, a lot!" I noticed that one guy seemed out of the loop about the quip. So I said "That's Shakespeare. 'What's in a name' is a famous line from Shakespeare." So he still looked perplexed and asked "From what?" And although I knew it was from *Romeo and Juliet*, I said, "Look it up. You might learn some interesting things along the way."

I'm not proposing that you spend years studying Shakespeare, but a topical knowledge of certain things will greatly enhance your capabilities for dealing in the major leagues with people who are well educated in a variety of subjects. Don't be left out! Take a few hours a week to review the classics in literature or history or something outside of your usual range of interests. Limiting yourself is not the best choice. Many topics come up in the course of a business discussion or interview, and while we can't know everything, we should know as much as we can.

Abraham Lincoln's statement at the beginning of this essay sums up what I'm trying to get across to you. It also incorporates Huxley's statement about being teachable. An added bonus to this attitude is that it will keep you young. Being a know-it-all will age you before your time, in addition to making you unteachable, so avoid those pitfalls. And building connected thoughts? Whoever thought that Abraham Lincoln and Aldous Huxley could be so connected? This essay proved that they could be, and we didn't need any dots to help us—just brain power and the attempt at building bridges between eras, cultures, backgrounds, and civilizations. Let that be an example of how to bridge your own gaps and to get yourself where you want to go. Creative thinking is a must these days. Make it work for you.

Fear defeats more people than any
other one thing in the world.

—Ralph Waldo Emerson

To ask the right question is already
half the solution of a problem.

—Carl Jung

Confronting
Your Fears

Recently, an interviewer asked me what my greatest fears were. I said I didn't have any. He seemed surprised, but this is how I see it: If you label something as a fear, then it creates fear when sometimes it's not a fear but a concern. For example, I know just as well as everyone else that New York City experienced a major terrorist attack and the thought of that is a concern for all of us, because it affects all of us. It's happened in many places, so it's a worldwide concern. But if we let it become a firmly rooted fear, the terrorists will have won.

The same applies to business. Do you fear owning a business? Translate that for yourself as asking: Are you concerned about owning a business yourself? Why? What specifically are those concerns?

It's much easier to break down a concern than it is a fear. Fear creates a block that will only hinder your creative thinking. Objectivity will remove that block and allow for creative ideas to flow.

An antidote to fear is as simple as problem solving. Whether you have investing, estate planning, or running a business on your mind, or all of those things, they can be broken down into units of thought and dealt with in an orderly manner. It's a bit like a jigsaw puzzle—you need to find the right place for each piece of the puzzle until the whole is apparent.

When I began to construct Trump Tower, for example, I had several things in mind that I knew I wanted. I wanted a certain kind of marble called Breccia Perniche, which was expensive, beautiful, and rare. It was also irregular and had white spots and white veins, which bothered me, so I went to the quarry itself and marked off the best slabs with black tape. Action turned this concern into a problem solved. I got exactly the marble pieces I wanted, and sitting around worrying about whether those pieces would be right or wrong was getting me nowhere. As a result of deciding to go to the quarry myself, the pieces of this puzzle fell into place and the finished product was perfect.

Know that if you want to own your own business, you will be doing a lot of the work yourself. That's just the way it is. It isn't all about giving orders or having other people do the legwork or brainwork for you. That comes into the picture, but you should always be ready to go at it yourself. If that idea bothers you, maybe you'd be better off being an employee. If responsibility comes naturally to you, or if you enjoy that challenge, owning your own business is a good fit.

Fear has a way of making things bigger than they are. There's an old German proverb to the effect that "fear makes the wolf bigger than he is," and that is true. But the opposite of fear is faith, which is one reason you've got to believe in yourself and see yourself as victorious. You will know you are capable of dealing with any discouragements, bullies, or problems along the way.

When I was faced with some huge debts in the early 1990s, it was widely reported that I was finished, done for, gone. Looking at the numbers alone made that seem clear to the media. However, I never believed I was finished. I simply saw that situation as a problem I had to solve and went about doing that. I'm not saying it was easy, because it wasn't. It was a big problem. But I refused to give in to fear or to believe what was being said about my so-called demise. I came back to become more successful than I ever was, and that's why I believe business is very much about problem solving. If you can learn to deal with and solve problems, you will have a much bigger margin for success.

Do not allow fear to settle into place in any part of your life. It is a defeating attitude and a negative emotion. Recognize and zap it immediately. Replace it with a problem-solving attitude, faith in yourself, and hard work. Put that formula into working order for yourself and you'll be dealing from a position of power, not fear. That's winning.

*People with vision master the ability to see
through to the heart of issues and investments.
They value transparency.*

—ROBERT KIYOSAKI

~~~❧~~~

Imagination: A Key
to Financial Savvy

I have the great advantage of having graduated from the Wharton School of Business, which is probably the best in the world. They made sure we were well versed in everything having to do with business. This is not always a guarantee of success, but at least we were well equipped for it.

Having had this advantage, I will explain a few things for those who haven't. Finance and business is a complex mix of components that embraces a large spectrum of enterprises. It's like having a technique and then being able to apply it to different mediums. As a builder, I instinctively saw the different aspects of finance fitting and falling into place in a large blueprint—and as I learned more, those blueprints became larger and larger. When I look back, I realize I was thinking big way back in school.

This might sound simplistic, but I'm a firm believer in visualization, and it worked for me. A blueprint might not work for you, but they are something I was familiar with. It might be a Miró painting or some other design or sculpture that works for you. I've heard some interesting stories of what people visualized on their path to success. One person used a photograph of bread and salt as his inspiration, and he became vastly successful. To each his own on this one.

Some financial courses are dry—but necessary. I was able to handle them by making them more interesting in my own mind by applying the principles immediately to some imaginary project I would come up with. By doing this, I was already working in the real world while I was in school, which I think saved me a lot of time when I actually got started on my own. I had been multitasking before I knew what multitasking was.

In reviewing my career, I think this aspect of my approach, on top of having the foundation of great schooling, is largely responsible for my success. I didn't realize I was doing it until much later, when I would somehow know how things worked or where things went in the big picture of any project I might be considering or actively involved in. I had already been working on it years before, and while I still encountered problems, things would somehow fall into place as they should. It's one way of being prepared.

A lot of people have imagination, but it doesn't help them because they can't execute. I'm able to execute with the imagination. Make sure your foundation is there to begin with and then grow from there in your imagination. That's how vision and transparency work together—and results can be remarkable.

Everyone who got where he is
has had to begin where he was.

—Robert Louis Stevenson

Is Business
Success a
Natural Talent?

A lot of people think I'm a natural at business. In some ways they might be right, but it's also an acquired skill that takes discipline and focus, just as being an athlete or a musician takes perseverance and years of training. Before I decided to go to the Wharton School of Finance, I had thought about attending the University of Southern California to study film, but once I decided on Wharton, I was a very serious and focused business student.

There's a certain amount of bravado in what I do these days, and part of that bravado is to make it look easy. That's why I've often referred to business as being an art. I've always liked Andy Warhol's statement that, "making money is art and working is art and good business is the best art." I agree.

I received a star on the Hollywood Walk of Fame in January of 2007, which was a big surprise for someone who opted for Wharton and real estate as a career. Did I have a natural talent for the entertainment industry? Maybe, but I've also always paid attention to it. I understand how it operates, and I'm always learning. When I was in school, I always did more than was expected and studied on my own in addition to what was required. I've noticed that a lot of very successful people have done the same thing, no matter what their respective fields might be.

Winston Churchill was known for being a great orator, and I remember thinking he must have been born with this talent until I read about him and discovered he spent a great deal of time developing this skill. It wasn't just a natural ability—he worked at it constantly. His talent was the result of deliberate and focused work. Mozart studied music at an unusually early age, and his aptitude was obviously there, but that aptitude was carefully developed.

The natural ability I may have as a businessman is being able to see the big picture while I'm taking care of a lot of details. I can focus on a few things at once at this point and find them working themselves out. That comes with experience, but I remember making a deliberate attempt to assimilate as much as possible at all times, even back in school.

Some people are visionaries. Bill Gates is an example, as is Mark Burnett, but they are also very good businessmen. So where does talent come in? Some people just seem to have an edge for what they do, like Tiger Woods or Roger Federer in sports. There are prodigies, it seems, but under close scrutiny all prodigies were carefully trained. I think talent has to do with aptitude for what you are doing. Some people are simply doing the wrong thing, and when they find the right thing, they become successful. Working hard and working intelligently should go together.

Heredity and environment are two factors that I consider seriously, from personal experience. My father was a great example: He was in the construction and real estate industry, and I saw firsthand what it took to succeed. I had no delusions of it being an easy or glamorous path. I chose to make it more glamorous because my tastes went toward that aesthetic. I consider myself very fortunate to have had this education from my father from an early age. I believe it gave me a great advantage, and I often say that I'm a member of the lucky sperm club.

But did it give me a natural talent? I don't think so. It gave me an advantage that I deliberately chose to develop into an advantage. You can be around something and either have no interest or aptitude for it, so it wouldn't be of any help to you. My elder brother had no interest in real estate and decided to do something else. I had a friend who worked on Wall Street because everyone in his family did, but he was a disaster. All the familiar indications were there for his success, but he wasn't suited for it, and not until he left and did something else did he become successful.

When I started to develop golf courses, I had a lot to learn. I loved the game and knew golf courses as a player, but developing a golf course is another story. I consulted with the world's experts before I started out. My golf courses have won awards for their beauty, but it wasn't a natural talent I had as a developer. My advantage is that I had a passion for the game and wanted the most beautiful courses possible to be realized.

There has been research done on cross training your brain, and they mention how you can transfer the skills developed to enhance your performance in other areas. That's one reason I have always encouraged people to golf—it's a brain game and it works on several levels. I've gotten a lot of great ideas and solutions to problems during a golf game, so I readily endorse this theory. It works. It might be painting or playing the piano that works for you, but it gives credibility to the developing of a hobby or outside interest that will complement your business bent.

I've also come to believe in luck. I've known people who have worked hard and done everything to succeed, and yet it just doesn't seem to happen for them. I'm not sure what the concrete reasons might be, but it makes me believe in luck to a certain extent. It's also true that not everyone can be wildly successful. Maybe it's just a balance in the world that we can't always control. But I've noticed that it helps to believe you're lucky, because luck will seem to favor you.

Business is about creativity. That's where the art part comes in. Every industry has its leaders, and if I'm known in real estate, it is because I approach my work cognitively as well as creatively. Peter Gelb, the general manager at the Metropolitan Opera, is really putting the opera back on the map by applying contemporary marketing ideas to this venerable institution. He is promoting it in ways that today's market can absorb and appreciate. You have to be alert for ways of revitalizing the old and creating the new, or combining them, to achieve the best results.

It was decades ago that I bought the deserted rail yards along the Hudson River, and today Trump Place is nearing completion—eighteen beautiful buildings, a park, and a pier that have enhanced Manhattan's West Side. Sometimes people think things just happen overnight, but that's not always the case, even if you are well known and well established. Success is often a matter of patience, and patience can be developed if you don't have it naturally.

In summation, is business success a natural talent? I think it's a combination of aptitude, work, and luck.

He who will not economize
will have to agonize.

—CONFUCIUS

Keep It Short,
Fast, and Direct

When Confucius mentions "agonize" in his quote, I have to tell you that I can relate. As someone on the receiving end of conversations with people who do not know how to edit themselves, I can understand what agony means. I don't mean to be impolite, but I am often thinking to myself, "how long is it going to take for this person to get to the point? We could've flown to Australia by now and they're still in the middle of take-off." Business is no place for stream of consciousness babbling, no matter how colorful you might think you're being. Whatever you're doing, keep it short, fast, and direct. It's also more polite. Most people don't have time to waste. I realize that Confucius was referring to the noneconomizer, and they will suffer, too, but why make everyone miserable by being unnecessarily chatty?

I mentioned in my book *Think Like a Billionaire* that Ricardo Bellino had exactly three minutes to give me his business presentation. I was extremely busy that day and not particularly in the mood for a presentation, so I thought he might decline, which would free up my day a bit. Not only did he not decline, he gave me such a great presentation within those three minutes that we did a deal together. It's surprising what people can do with a deadline.

I mention that because sometimes we have to give ourselves deadlines. Practice giving your presentation in under five minutes. Practice giving your introduction in less than three minutes. You will discover that you can be an effective editor by cutting out everything that isn't absolutely necessary. Your audience, or your superiors, will be grateful for your ability to distill the essence for them.

We probably all know what it's like to receive junk mail. Sometimes there are piles of it waiting for us, and we have to sort through it all to get to the important stuff. Don't offer any junk mail to anyone—just give them the good stuff, or the necessary items. That can get you places far faster than you can imagine.

In that sense, business is often like a relay race. To have a tight team, a winning team, you can't have someone who lags behind, because everyone will suffer because of it. Make sure you're not the one who holds things up for everyone. Learn to sprint when it comes to being clear. Have a contest with yourself by asking, "How concise can I possibly be?" Then best yourself every time. Get to the essence immediately.

Someone who analyzed my negotiating technique said I had an advantage over most people because I had the ability to get to the point faster than anybody else. While they were still formulating their sentences, I'd already written the book. I already had the deal done in my head. That ability didn't happen overnight—I've worked at it for a long time. But we can all put that technique to work every day, whether it's relaying a message to someone, writing a letter, or ordering lunch.

Those of you who have watched *The Apprentice* will notice that the candidates who can present the facts with the least amount of verbal decoration will have an advantage. Listening to a five-minute explanation that can be easily edited to thirty seconds automatically sends a red alert to me and my advisors. We don't have the time for loquacious colleagues, and the longwinded diatribes we often have to suffer through will greatly diminish their chances of winning.

Simple as it sounds, there is great wisdom in the short, fast, and direct route. Knowing where you're going in your conversation and demonstrating to others you know where you're going by being concise, is a big step toward leadership and respect. Hone these skills in every situation and with every opportunity you have, whether you're in line at the corner deli or in the boardroom on *The Apprentice.* Learn to economize. People appreciate brevity in today's world.

Don't find fault.
Find a remedy.

—HENRY FORD

∼◡

Have the
Right Mindset
for the Job

When I think of work, I often see it as problem solving. I've said before that if you don't have problems, then either you're pretending not to see something or you don't run your own business. Problems come with the territory, and they should never surprise you. You should expect them.

Even if you work for someone else, it's a good idea to expect problems and to be ready for them. To me it's a realistic approach. No matter how hard you work, there are times that things happen that are out of our control. Keep your eyes on your ideals as well as reality. That's what being prepared really means.

Very often when people refer to the morning of September 11, 2001, they will mention that it was a beautiful September morning in New York City. Within two hours, our view of a beautiful morning had been radically changed. Were we prepared for it? Could we control the outcome?

That is an extreme example, but it helps to be in control of those things we *can* control. Every day ask yourself what problems might arise, review every project yourself, and make sure you are on top of your own agenda. Be as thorough as possible. Be alert. In business, there are no half-days or slow days. If there are, something's missing. Make it your business to find out what it is, and then do something about it. Find a remedy.

When I say have the right mindset, I am thinking about responsibility. People who take responsibility have no need to blame others or to be continually finding fault. These are the naysayers who never amount to much, and never manage to contribute much either. Don't join their club. They're the lowest common denominator.

I knew a guy that I used to call up just to see who and what he would be blaming that day. I don't think that guy ever made a single mistake in his entire life—from day one nothing was ever his fault. His biggest blind spot was himself, and sad to say, he eventually became a total loser because he never thought of the remedy for his many failures: himself. Look at yourself first when things go wrong.

I've been in business long enough now, and have had ups and downs, so I can go from seeing the problem to seeing the solution rather quickly. Don't emphasize the problem so much—emphasize the solution. It's a mindset that works, and it's one way to accentuate the positive without being blind to the negative.

Another tip for those of you who work for someone else: While you may be budding entrepreneurs, there is great value to being able to be an effective and efficient team player. If you have watched *The Apprentice,* you will notice that the people without team skills don't do so well. Yes, each person wants to win, but part of the game, and an important part, is to work well with your team. It's something that will be noticed in any work environment. Can you employ out-of-the-box thinking while remaining within the constraints of team effort?

I've also noticed how much time *The Apprentice* teams spend bickering and infighting, which is not only a waste of precious time, but annoying and sometimes even embarrassing. These people are highly qualified, and to see and hear them carrying on at length, many times over inconsequential things, is a clear indication that they should heed Henry Ford's advice about finding a remedy instead of finding fault.

Give your full attention to your work! I'm constantly surprised by people who don't seem to have this ability. That's why you hear me emphasizing focus so much—it's absolutely necessary in order to achieve results. *Mindset includes responsibility and focus.* We all know how to turn on the television set. Be equally adept at turning on your mind to matters at hand and you might surprise yourself by what you can accomplish.

The beginning of wisdom
is a definition of terms.

—SOCRATES

~~~

Momentum Is Something You Have to Work at to Maintain

Socrates lived a long time ago, but he came up with some good ones. For example, a definition of terms could be another way of saying "negotiation" or it could mean the definition of a word or simply the wisdom of being concise. But just as negotiation takes practice, so does momentum. You don't do one great deal and then think that every deal you subsequently make will automatically be great. You don't get a great rhythm going once and then think it will always be there. Even the greatest jazz musicians know there's a "zone" they're aiming for, and hopefully they'll get there. But they don't take it for granted that they will. They work at it every time they play.

Momentum comes in different forms, but its common denominator is energy. Some synonyms are power, force, strength, impetus, and drive—all good things for accomplishments of any sort. We've all heard of biorhythms and how we have high days and low days, but my approach to that is to design your own chart and then work at maintaining it. My biorhythms are always on full speed ahead. I've developed my stamina to keep up to that level, and the results are apparent at this point.

Many things become easier with practice and experience, and momentum is one of them. You can take advantage of this great energy source just by being aware that it exists. It's like swimming with the current versus being dragged down and out by a riptide. Find your own current and then go with it! Don't allow for distractions. Do everything you can to maintain your energy flow.

There was a hugely successful real estate developer that I admired very much, and then he went into a decline. We saw each other at a party, and I pointedly asked him what caused this to happen. He said, "Donald, I lost my momentum, and I couldn't get it back." When this guy fell, he fell hard. I learned a great lesson from him that night, so much so that I devoted a lot of time to studying and applying the power of momentum to my own life and business. I didn't ever want that to happen to me, and I repeat this story for a reason. The lesson applies whether you're in real estate or not.

I see people who get in their own way when it comes to momentum. I knew a guy who would take ten big fast steps forward and then sit there, like he'd reached a plateau, and would expect things to just keep moving forward. It doesn't work that way! Maybe he liked the rollercoaster approach to business, but he literally wore himself out before he had enough substantial success to see him through, and his ups and down didn't work out on the balance sheet in the long run. Watch out for streaks of momentum that you can't sustain—keep your equilibrium in all things, even in your energy output.

There's a *Newsweek* ad from the late '80s in which they have a photograph of me with the caption, "Few things in life are as brash as *Newsweek*." I don't mind being called brash because to me it's being bold, it's having energy, it's getting things done. But there are constraints to be considered, and my momentum is carefully monitored. I'm not exactly brash in that sense, but I know you can't get things done if you're too timid. My persona will never be one of the wallflower—I'd rather build walls than cling to them.

Socrates said things that can make us think. So here's another take on the quote that opened this essay: Maybe he's advising us to define our own terms. Maybe he's suggesting that we start thinking for ourselves. Maybe what he's suggesting is actually very wise advice. In that case, my advice to you regarding momentum is definitive: Get yours going!

~~⌒⌒

Learn from
Setbacks
and Mistakes

How we handle difficult situations in life says a lot about who we are. How we view them is also an important element in how we will deal with adversity. Some events will wipe out one person but will make another person even more tenacious. That's why I always ask myself, "Is this a blip, or is it a catastrophe?"—it gives me a point of reason in the midst of bad news.

You've heard me talk about passion before, how it's a necessary ingredient for success. Reason is also necessary, and when we experience setbacks and mistakes, that can be a good time to employ reason or objectivity. It also sets us up to learn something from the experience. It's like the old saying about when one door closes, another door opens—I see it as meaning there's another chance, another opportunity waiting. But we have to be open to it. I've known some people who could be staring at an open door and not even realize it's open, let alone its significance.

I can remember when things turned around for me in a big way, and what I learned is that you have to maintain your focus at all times—and your momentum. You've heard me mention those two success tips before, and this is because I learned about them the hard way—I'd lost my focus and suddenly I was faced with some setbacks. But here's another thought: Your problems can be temporary if you keep your momentum moving forward. We all experience difficulties, but they can be blips if you remain positive and move on.

When I decide to do something, I have enough experience to expect problems. Rarely is anything worth doing just a breeze. Sometimes I feel like Sisyphus, who was condemned to ceaselessly rolling a stone uphill—but that's just the way it is sometimes. So I just keep going. I don't give up. My focus is intense enough to make the effort worth it, and my momentum makes sure that my efforts won't be futile. I have learned a lot because of demanding situations.

One way to avoid mishandling mistakes is to realize they can happen to us every day. It's a way of being prepared without being a pessimist. Problems, setbacks, mistakes, and losses are all a part of life. It's something we have to accept. We shouldn't be shocked if and when they happen. Don't let things knock you off your feet or off your rocker either. Keep your equilibrium by knowing what you're dealing with. If you are taken by surprise, then by all means, ask yourself what you've learned from the experience. Don't just go out and make the same mistake again and hope for the best. You'll be getting a lot of the same hard knocks and tough lessons over and over again if you don't assess your situation each and every time.

Here's where the going gets tricky. You have to know when to call it quits and when to keep moving forward. There's always that fine line between acceptance and resignation to think about.

Sometimes it's not so fine—as when you find out someone is a scoundrel and nothing's going to change them. Then it's wise to call it quits with them. Other times, we have to realize that everyone makes mistakes and to try to be a little more accepting of that fact. Just as you don't want to give up on yourself, you can't always just give up on other people either. That's where experience and discernment will come in. But what's most important is to never give up on yourself. You never know when the tide is going to turn in your favor, providing you have been paying attention and working toward something worthwhile.

There was a time, early in my real estate career, when I was trying to get a deal done and I thought I'd endured and worked through every obstacle possible. Wrong. It took me two months more of hammering away at the details until I arrived at what was considered a done deal. Had I known what I was going to have to go through from the beginning, I'm not sure I would have had the fortitude to go for it or to stick it out. But I'm glad I did. It was my first big success, which was the renovation of the Grand Hyatt Hotel at Grand Central. Did I learn a lot? You bet I did. Every setback gave me a great lesson, and I was becoming a very educated man in the process.

You have to be the same way, and you *can* be the same way. Just be tough, be strong, be willing to learn—and you will learn. So don't be afraid of mistakes or setbacks. They can be your learning tools on the way to building something great for yourself. We all have something to learn today. Remember that and your chances for success will increase dramatically.

A man cannot be comfortable
without his own approval.

—MARK TWAIN

Tell People
About
Your Success

I have a friend who is extremely accomplished and also extremely wealthy. Uber-wealthy, as they say. But one day he called me up to see if I could get him reservations at Jean Georges Restaurant and I had to ask myself, "What's the point of his immense success if he can't even get a reservation in New York?" The only reason he can't is because no one has ever heard about him. He's shy about using his name, to the extent that it serves him no good. He has to call other people, like me, to help him out.

That got me to thinking about the toot-your-own-horn theory, which is something I believe in. Here's a perfect example of why I believe in it. This poor rich guy might as well be just a poor guy when trying to get in the right places. The power of a name can be incredible. It can open doors like nothing else. A lot of people might have been richer than Aristotle Onassis, but when people heard the name Onassis, they knew who he was. I've mentioned before that one of the perks of being famous is being able to get restaurant reservations without any problem. My uber-rich friend has not entitled himself to very many perks.

Ever notice if you introduce someone and then later add on something like, "as you know, he won the Pulitzer prize," that the reaction to the person becomes entirely different? It goes from polite to excited in no time flat. Suddenly the nobody is a some-body. Suddenly their PR power, or their buzz effect, has escalated. But unless you have someone around to toot your horn for you, you'll have to get accustomed to doing it for yourself. The well-established brand name literally speaks for itself. Some people may not even like the designs Karl Lagerfeld comes up with for Chanel, but because it says Chanel, they'll buy them, wear them, and love them.

A name can speak volumes, but until you have a "household name" you might do well to tell people who you are and what you've done. It's a start. It's also a way of networking to find out if you might have common interests. Can you imagine if Luciano Pavarotti had been singing, contentedly, in some obscure place his whole life, what we would have missed? Or if Elton John was happy to just sing for himself in a garage somewhere? There's nothing wrong with bringing your talents to the surface.

Having an ego and acknowledging it is a healthy choice. Our ego is the center of our consciousness and gives us a sense of pur-pose. People with no ego will have very little life force, and peo-ple with too much will tend toward dictatorial personalities. As with everything, keeping a good balance is important. Your ego can serve to keep your momentum moving forward. It can keep you vibrant and productive. It can keep your focus where it should be, which is on your work. After awhile, you won't have to tell people about your success because they'll already know about it. Do not disregard your ego.

It's very important to be your own best friend. As Mark Twain put it, be comfortable with your own approval. A lot of times, people will enjoy belittling your accomplishments as well as your ambitions. If you are steadfast in your self-respect, that will not even bother you because you will be able to see those people as the small fries that they are. Critics serve their own purpose, and that's fine, because you'll be smart enough to serve your own purpose, too. Think about it: If you can't say great things about yourself, who do you think will? So don't be afraid to toot your own horn when you've done something worth tooting about. Let's end with another statement from Mark Twain: "I am opposed to millionaires, but it would be dangerous to offer me the position."

The best vision is insight.

—MALCOLM FORBES

~~◦

Prescience

P*rescience* is a word that defines vision, foresight, creative discernment, or perception. I have often been called a visionary, but not until 2006 was I noted for having prescience. The same day as the book launch party in Trump Tower for my book with Robert Kiyosaki, *Why We Want You To Be Rich,* which was October 12, 2006, was also the day the Nobel Committee announced the 2006 Nobel Prize winner in literature. What does that have to do with me? Well, I was getting calls and letters of congratulations for having the "prescience" to recognize the Nobel winner's talent before the Nobel Committee did. This came as a surprise to me—that people would remember my letter to the *New York Times* in 2005 in which I mentioned the very gifted writer Orhan Pamuk (along with John Updike and Philip Roth) as being an example of what a great writer should be. Pamuk won the Nobel Prize that day, and considering he wasn't exactly a household name, people were suddenly saying I had prescience.

Sometimes we just have perceptions about certain people or things, and this was one of those times. Did I know he was going to win the Nobel Prize? No, but his talent was certainly developed enough to make him a contender, and I might have bet on it. I've written before about using your gut instincts, and sometimes that's what prescience or foresight is. It's a valuable ability, especially in business, and it's worth giving it some thought.

More recently, we experienced a historic day in the financial sector. What happened on Wall Street was unprecedented, and it was rightly called "the shock market" in mid-September of 2008. Neal Cavuto asked me to make a comment about it, and he found footage of an appearance I'd made on his show eight months prior to this debacle in which I'd predicted something similar happening. I had seen the indications that we might be entering a very difficult phase. Is this ESP? No, it's just paying attention on a daily basis and looking into the future a bit. That's insight and foresight working together.

We all have hidden areas of expertise. I may have instincts when it comes to real estate, but I have also spent many years developing them. Your instincts may be more acute in another area. There's nothing wrong with very solid knowledge and experience to go along with our perceptions. In fact, that is when you will be playing with a very full deck. Experience, knowledge, and prescience are a formidable combination of powers. Do not underestimate any of them.

I am more concerned with
my money being returned than
the return on my money.

—MARK TWAIN

~~~

The Shock
Market

W hat transpired on Wall Street on September 15, 2008, is one day for the history books. I had predicted this would happen about two years ago and again about eight months ago when I appeared on Neal Cavuto's show. That the landscape of Wall Street could be altered this rapidly is something we should think about. September 15, 2008, was the worst day on Wall Street since right after the 9/11 attacks, with a fallout of some financial giants that we thought were untouchable.

Here's my view of this situation. We survived and prospered after 9/11, and we will do the same this time. The components are different, but I believe the government is doing the right thing with this financial mess. They have worked hard and long, but a mess is a mess. I won't equivocate on that. I saw the indications that the world was in for a tough period of time, so I can't say I'm terribly surprised.

Here are some points to consider. The price of oil, which is the life blood of all economies, is down. That's good news. I've already written about that subject and about the many tankers full of oil treading water and going nowhere.

Out of chaos comes reinvention. That can be a good thing, although it won't be easy. There appears to have been a lack of balance, and this is one way of starting something new that might be more effective. Necessity creates a place for creativity, and having the facility to implement a plan B strategy is something everyone should strive for. I've learned that having a plan B is common sense. We'll just have to come up with one, and it could eventually be better than what we've had.

As a Manhattan real estate developer, my observation is that there will be more people looking for jobs than will be looking for apartments. That's not great news for the real estate market in New York City, but it's not dire. A lot of things are and will continue to be changing, in our country as well as around the world. There is a well-known Greek motto that I think is pertinent to today's economic situation: "The sea gets sick but never dies." The Greeks have been around for a long time and they've watched the ebb and flow of history for many centuries.

Remember that things are cyclical, so be resilient, be patient, be creative, and remain positive. Reinvention can be a good thing for everyone.

Wealth is the product of
man's capacity to think.

—AYN RAND

~~~

Financial
Literacy

Financial literacy is financial intelligence. Robert Kiyosaki, the author of *Rich Dad Poor Dad*, explains how he learned about money from two father figures, his poor dad and his rich dad. He had a mentor who explained how money works, and since his own father was highly educated but poor, the lessons were brought to light in a very tangible way for him. If you haven't read *Rich Dad Poor Dad* or *Cashflow Quadrant*, I would suggest that you do. He has very sound advice that can make a big difference in your quality of life and your approach to money.

The reason we wrote *Why We Want You To Be Rich* is because the more independent people become, the stronger a nation becomes as a whole. As we've noticed with the recent upheaval on Wall Street, things aren't always as solid as they seem. That calls for individual responsibility and financial intelligence. We can't rely on systems to do the work for us or expect things to fall in place because the people who are smart about money are supposedly working there. I have always been wary of the stock market. It's a gamble, but it can be lucrative, which is the lure.

In short, there are no guarantees. That means being alert to national and world markets. Do your homework daily. I shouldn't need to emphasize this if you've paid attention to what's transpired in the United States from 2006 until now, which is late 2008. There was an implosion in the financial sector that was unprecedented in our history. I see it as a wake-up call.

Robert and I tried to warn people back in 2006. Now I'm back to tell you loud and clear that this area of your life is of great importance. Yes, study your specific area of interest diligently, but realize that if there is no money for scholarships, whether you are studying anthropology or literature or law, you might be out of luck. Everyone will be affected. Whatever your emphasis of study is, be aware of what is going on financially around the world.

We are all businessmen and women, whether you see it that way yet or not. If you like art and can't make money at it, you eventually realize that everything is business, even your art. That's why I like Warhol's statement about good business being the best art. It's a fact. That's also another reason I see my business as an art and so I work at it passionately.

We all have opinions. Due diligence means finding out the difference between opinions and facts. I was astounded to find out how many people don't know how the financial world is set up. Equities, emerging markets, asset management, commodities, mutual funds, hedge funds, annuities, stocks, bonds, and mortgages should be common knowledge by the time you are in high school. That's a big oversight in our educational system. Every student should know how they all work and never expect a financial "expert" to give them the whole story. You have to know it yourself.

This is a capitalistic society, which is good, but it also means watching out for yourself.

My advice to you is to take as many finance classes as you can, no matter what your line of work is and/or your focus of study might be. If you're not good at economics or statistics, all the more reason to take those classes and pay attention. Having a financial blind spot is setting yourself up for some unpleasant surprises in the future. Know how the financial sector works. It affects you in every way.

I heard someone say during the amazing collapse of some financial giants in the United States, that, "I'm not really interested in the market." Oh really?! I was stunned. As if it doesn't affect them! When they don't have a job to go to next week, maybe they'll realize they should be interested. The ripple effect is felt everywhere, nationally and internationally, when the markets and banks falter. It shows we are all connected, whether we want to believe that or not.

My emphasis here is to advise you to be financially literate. It's in your best interest in the biggest sense you can imagine. Please heed my advice and pay attention. You can start by clicking onto the Finance page on Yahoo! when you go onto your computer every day. Check out the markets a few times a day and see how the dollar is doing against the Euro and Yen. Learn to read the charts and the trends. Read the pertinent articles. That's a baby step, but it will get you thinking on the right wavelength—which could make a significant difference in your quality of life.

A hungry man will realize something immediately. If he had money, he wouldn't be hungry. That's a very basic visual, but it applies. In other words, pay attention to your financial literacy.

Every individual has a place
to fill in the world and is important, in some respect,
whether he chooses to be so or not.

—NATHANIEL HAWTHORNE

Destiny

When I was going through my mail one day, I came across a stack of letters from students in middle school about *The Apprentice* and the business lessons they've learned from watching it. There must have been forty letters, so I skimmed through them, and a couple questions stood out because they were asked repeatedly. One was about how to achieve success, and the other one was how to deal with obstacles on the way to success.

My first thought was how important planning ahead is to success, and how equally important it is to remain flexible with those plans. How do you tell students about the importance of plans and sticking to them while still emphasizing the necessity for flexibility? It would seem to be a contradiction.

There's a quote I like by an anonymous thinker: "The bend in the road is not the end of the road unless you refuse to take the turn." That's a valuable thought for business skills as well as life skills. Very rarely does everything work out the way we hope or think it will. In fact, sometimes it works out better when you've had to take a few detours along the way, but what will help you the most is to be prepared for them. Interesting things have happened to people when they've taken side trips, planned or otherwise.

I was scheduled to make a short appearance on a boat in New York City and then to get off before it took an evening long cruise around Manhattan. The boat was full of happy and excited people, and the festivities were just starting to begin, but I had other plans in midtown, and I was getting ready to leave when I noticed that the boat had already left the dock and was in the middle of the river. I wasn't too happy about this turn of events, but there wasn't much I could do about it except to adjust my mood and accept a cruise around my favorite city as an unexpected adventure. What happened is that I had the opportunity to talk with a variety of people while having some great ideas at the same time. New York City is beautiful when it's lit up at night and it turned out to be a very pleasant evening for everyone. If I had perceived the situation as a misadventure, I don't think I would have had some of the creative ideas that came to me, or as much fun.

This is a simple example of an unanticipated event that turned into a positive memory. I had plans that were business related that had to be changed, but it wasn't the end of the world. It was a blip, not a catastrophe. When these things happen to you, whether they be big or small events, remember that your perception of their magnitude will play a big part in what you can reap from them. We've all heard the term "go with the flow," and in my case, that's what I had to do unless I wanted to jump overboard and attempt to swim the Hudson River at night. Sometimes common sense will intervene, too.

Carefully planning your way to success is a sure way to achieve your goals, and that approach should never be underestimated. Just remember that you need to be patient and persevering and to know that there can be delays and detours along the way. I've waited twenty years to see some things happen, but it was worth the wait and I had to change course a few times until the pieces finally fell into place. Destiny has a part to play in your life and in your business—so give it a chance to work.

What lies behind us
and what lies before us
are tiny matters compared
to what lies within us.

—RALPH WALDO EMERSON

~∽

Each Success Is the Beginning of the Next One

That thought by Ralph Waldo Emerson has always been an inspiration to me. It gives me energy to keep going full force because I know I still have a lot to accomplish. No matter what I may have achieved—or plan to achieve—I know it's "a tiny matter" compared to what I am capable of doing. Think about it: How can we be complacent with that kind of thought pattern going on? It would be impossible!

When I hear people say things like, "It's impossible to do more!" I always smile to myself and think, "I've just started!"—and it's just a great way to feel. I'd like you to have that feeling, too, because it's like having stepping stones in all the right places just waiting for you to see them.

Sometimes it helps to minimize your achievements to yourself so that you will be eager to do more. It's like saying, "Yeah, that was good, but I'm just getting warmed up" as a way to keep yourself challenged. The best achievers are those who are self-motivated, who are naturally curious, and who don't need to be told what to do next. Strive to be that kind of person. Entrepreneurs are driven by their own inner forces, and it's a great way of life as well as a great approach to life.

What lies within us? Hopefully, a lot of great ideas and plans for the future as well as the innate sense of our ability to achieve them. I think Emerson was alluding to this idea of hope in his statement. It's important for survival and it's important for success. Sometimes it is what keeps us going when the odds may not be on our side. Don't underestimate the power of some of the unseen or intangible forces in your life. Just because you can't see something doesn't mean it's not there. The first person to give you a chance should be yourself.

So give yourself a chance—every single day. Some people really are their own worst enemy. Don't fall into that abyss—because that's really what it is. Ever watched children when they are trying something new? They are excited, they are eager, and they welcome the challenge. That's an attitude to recapture or to try to emulate. The enthusiasm that discovery provides is a sure way to make sure that everything you are doing is paving the way toward your current as well as future successes. I received a letter from my kindergarten teacher, and she mentioned that what she remembers most clearly about me is that I never stopped asking questions. I wrote back to her and informed her that some things never change—that I still ask a lot of questions. But I said that it had obviously served me well, and I thanked her, belatedly, for her patience many years ago. Every one of my questions was the beginning of the next one.

So here's one for you: If you had nothing at all to do, what would you do? And after you did that, what would you do? And after you did that, what would be next on your list? I call that multithinking versus multitasking. Most people have at least a few things they want to do. Sometimes one thing leads to another—that's a form of discovery. Discovery breeds discovery, as in success breeds success. Quest-ions are thoughts with a quest.

Can you guess what the quest is? Knowledge. Knowledge is power. That's one reason you're reading this essay. No one is born a know-it-all. Wouldn't that be a little boring? I think it might be. Fortunately, at this time in history, things are moving so quickly that no one has the right to boredom. Just keeping up is the challenge we all have today. I like that challenge, because a challenge equals a success just waiting to happen.

Let's end this with a few good questions: What lies behind you? (What are your life experiences and education up to this point?) What lies before you? (What are your goals, your plans, your aspirations?) What lies within you? (Do you have what it takes to succeed? Do you know the full extent of your abilities yet? Do you know what the future holds for you? Do you know how your dreams will evolve?) Let's admit it—life is full of mystery. That includes *your* life, which is no tiny matter. So don't sell yourself short on something that important. Today is just the beginning.

Learning without thought
is labor lost.

—CONFUCIUS

~⁓

There Are Times
When You Should
Move On

Sometimes we have to be patient and sometimes we have to get moving. Wisdom is knowing which time is which and when to do what. I know, easier said than done. But we all know when we've exhausted certain possibilities—and quite possibly ourselves—in the course of finding out. Wouldn't it be great to know everything first?

That could save a lot of time. One way is to train your brain to do some assessing first. Do the "scenario" test: What if I quit this job, what would tomorrow bring? Maybe some adventures, but without a paycheck. What if I stayed in this job? The same old stuff but with a paycheck. What if I thought about a new career? A good plan, because you can stay in your job while you're working your brain toward something more challenging. Sometimes that will even open up opportunities in your present job. Do the brain work first, asking yourself a lot of questions.

If, at the end of trying to make your current situation better, it is an obvious dead end, then it's a good time to move on. Maybe it's just not a good fit. It's like a relationship—on paper all the important things seem to add up, but the chemistry just isn't there to make it work in reality. Jobs can be that way, too. Just as I've hired people with terrific credentials only to find out it's simply not a good match, for them or for me. You have to cut your losses quickly. That's a good thing to learn if you want to be successful.

When we hear of extremely successful people, it's usually safe to assume they've had some obstacles or difficulties along the way. There's a lot of trial and error before something is effortless or polished. Michelangelo said something worth thinking about: "If people only knew how hard I work to gain my mastery, it wouldn't seem so wonderful at all." The problem is, we usually only see the end result and not the process.

There was a guy who was a very successful businessman, but his first passion in life was the piano. He was very dedicated and disciplined, and he achieved a certain virtuosity, but he finally realized he would never be one of the greats. In other words, he knew he would never be a Horowitz or a Gould, and he had very high standards for himself. So he quit the piano and applied himself to business and he became enormously successful. He just knew he should move on, and he did. He remained a musician in his private life and maintained a healthy balance for himself with his interests. He said if he'd remained a pianist, he would have been frustrated. He did a lot of thinking before he made his move, but he knew it was the right decision.

It's not always easy to move on—it's leaving something behind in a way, but sometimes what's ahead will be better. We've got to do things we're suited for and hopefully that we enjoy. Success is a great feeling, and success should add to your health, not detract from it.

I sometimes tell people they are not cut out to be entrepreneurs because it's true. Some people are, and some people aren't. It will save you a lot of time and hardship if you can figure that out first. As with anything, you have to see how you handle pressure and the risk factor. It's similar to going through the set of questions we had at the beginning of this essay. Learn to scrutinize yourself and your capabilities, and find the time for some thought-provoking thinking. As Confucius said, "Learning without thought is labor lost." Don't let that apply to you. Learn, work, and think in equal proportions, and you'll be going in the right direction.

Men are born to succeed,
not fail.

—Henry David Thoreau

~⌒~

Keep the
Big Picture
in Mind

Sometimes people spend too much time focusing on problems instead of focusing on opportunities. You have to keep the big picture in mind even when minding the details or your vision could become micromanaged in an unnecessary way. I always try to keep two wavelengths going at once, which prevents brain cramps and reminds me that I'm destined for success. How do I know this destiny? Because like Thoreau, I believe we are born to succeed, not to fail. If I can believe it, you can believe it, too.

Here's how. First of all, expect problems. Even problems can be turned around to your advantage, and sometimes surprising events can happen. When I had some financial problems back in the 1990s, I remember debating with myself whether or not to attend a black tie dinner at the Waldorf. I certainly didn't feel like celebrating anything or talking to anyone, but I got dressed, went there, and as it turned out I was seated next to someone I really clicked with—and he was a banker. The chemistry for great things was there, and it was the last thing I had expected to happen. I had been in a negative mindset, but my disciplined side took over, and without any expectations on my part, things took a decidedly better turn just because I showed up.

Second, you have to remain determined. If you have a big picture in mind, you will need big determination to go with it. The old saying "Rome wasn't built in a day" is an apt one. There is no easy way—much as I'd like to tell you otherwise. But if you are doing something you love doing, it should not present too much hardship. Most of us are aware of the tremendous difficulties that faced people like Michelangelo and Beethoven, yet they prevailed and they're still with us centuries later. It helps to know what other people have faced in accomplishing their goals. A lot of times we don't know how much work is required until we get into something, no matter how much research we've done, so fortitude is absolutely necessary.

Then we come to the unexpected—events that happen that can thoroughly alter our plans, such as earthquakes, wars, natural disasters, and so forth. Here's when the theory of adaptability comes in. Are you able to remain flexible enough to handle catastrophes? Disasters happen, and they aren't always foreseen. Suddenly our big picture has a new script attached to it! Well, believe me, you can handle it if you go with the flow and remain determined at the same time. The best thing to remember here is Winston Churchill's advice to never give up: "Never, never, never, never, never, in nothing great or small, large or petty, never give in, except to convictions of honour and good sense. Never yield to force; never yield to the apparently overwhelming might of the enemy." We may not be experiencing the blitz, but sometimes when problems start up, it can feel like it. Prepare yourself with strength of character to withstand discouragements as well as disasters.

People who have endured great hardship often say they survived because they kept some sort of hope going, a vision of the future, despite horrible immediate circumstances. They may not have had a big picture in mind at the time, but they had a semblance of one. Try to emulate their example; it is obviously an effective thought process for survival. Sometimes a dead end can be a new beginning.

My father used to tell us this story he thought was really funny, although I never thought it was that funny. I think he was trying to tell us something about remaining determined. Anyway, it went like this: A guy loved soda. Just loved soda. So he decided to go into the business and named his product 3-Up. It was a failure. So he started over again and named his new product 4-Up. It, too, failed. So he started again and named his soda 5-Up. Once again, it failed. Once again, he tried again and named his soda 6-Up, and it, too, failed. Well, he decided he'd had it with the soda business, and he gave up. That was the end of my father's story! As we all knew, 7-Up became a very successful and famous brand of soda. So that must've been his message to us: The soda guy simply gave up too soon!

We've had some good examples, from Thoreau to Churchill to my father, so let's pay attention to them and keep them in mind in the years to come. I think it will do us all good.

Get the
Best People
You Can

O ne of the most important things I've learned is to watch what people do versus listening to what they say. Sometimes, judging on what I see them doing, I think people have no idea what they've talked about. It reminds me of a split personality, with the mouth going one way and everything else going the other way. One big step toward success is to get the two working in tandem. You will also find out that it will save you a lot of time and energy to become solid.

I've said before that every new hire is a gamble because you never know exactly what you're getting. Some people with great credentials don't deliver, and some people with not so great credentials turn out to be great. There is simply no guarantee when it comes to people, and watching them in action turns out to be the proving ground. That's why on *The Apprentice*, the candidates are told they are entering a job interview that will last for months.

It's a great way to see potential employees in action versus listening to how great they think they are.

One quality of leadership is knowing your subject. That also extends itself to knowing people. It's always a good idea to assume the worst, because then you might be pleasantly surprised. I've had some solid gold people and some real scoundrels, and somehow it manages to balance out. But my expectations are realistic—not every person is going to be a perfect match. And no matter how much you want to trust people, you still have to be a little paranoid.

That sounds tough—and it is—but never expect everything or everyone to be easy. To be blunt: We all have to watch out for ourselves. That includes you, and that includes me. It's best not to trust people too much, because that's just setting yourself up for some nasty surprises. I graduated from college in 1968, so I've had a fair share of experiences with people by now. If I were to tell you they were all great experiences, I'd be lying. I've met the gamut of personalities, and some of them had some disorders, to put it nicely. These disorders don't always surface quickly, so it's best to protect yourself from them to begin with. Be circumspect, if not paranoid, with people.

I've had people who have worked for me for over twenty-five or thirty years, so you may be wondering why I talk about being paranoid. It's another way of saying, "don't take anything for granted." I don't take my solid gold employees for granted because they don't take me for granted either. It's a two-way street and it works best that way. If you can aim for that, that's the best way to go. I have evidence that it can happen.

On the other hand, I've had some complete washouts, people who managed to prove themselves to be not only incompetent but untrustworthy. That's the other side you have to expect from time to time. To think it won't happen to you is a big take. I have been taken by surprise by certain unexpected behaviors, so now I rein in my expectations, and my equilibrium is the better for it. A leader needs to know about people to remain a leader.

Most of us have been exposed to the work of Shakespeare, and he spends a great deal of time dwelling on the characteristics of human nature. Some of the examples are extreme, but they aren't so far-fetched as to be unbelievable, or Shakespeare wouldn't still be performed today. There's something about his work that is timeless, and the timelessness comes from his insight into human nature. One of his greatest achievements was *King Lear*, which is a good lesson in how good intentions don't always work out for the best, and it becomes a virtual wipeout while showing the complexities of human relations. That's a dark example, but it's better to be aware than to be unaware of what the world can be like.

On the brighter side, I think most people want to be the best they can be. That's probably one reason you're reading this right now—you've chosen the high road, the path to more knowledge and experience. It's one of the reasons I enjoy giving speeches and teaching—I can share what I know with people who are really motivated to know more, to do more, and to improve the quality of their minds and lives. It's a great feeling. I hope you'll continue to expand your life every day.

It's not that I'm so smart,
it's just that I stay with problems longer.

—ALBERT EINSTEIN

~~~

Winners See Problems
as Just Another Way
to Prove Themselves

Problems are a mind exercise. Problems can be opportunities. If you put different names on different things, it's surprising how much that can affect your approach to them. Some people play chess. They see it as a game. It is also an art, a science, and an exercise in problem solving. But they enjoy it and are passionate about it. Bobby Fischer, the famed chess champion, answered when asked about his technique: "I don't believe in psychology. I believe in good moves." He also mentioned that he gave 98 percent of his mental energy to chess, whereas others gave only 2 percent. That explains his success. It couldn't be said—or done—more simply.

Maybe we're not all chess champions, but we can still learn a lot about problem solving. There's the old saying that if you don't have problems, then you don't have a job. They come with the territory of any endeavor. So it's good to know how to deal with the inevitable. If the sun rises and the sun sets, there will be problems to deal with. I know people who see problems as a game to be won. I know people who see problems as burdens. That's just giving yourself another problem to deal with.

We've all heard people talk about someone who has "a lot of baggage," meaning they're carrying around a lot of problems with them. That really isn't necessary, especially in this age when traveling light is the goal. Try to avoid the gravitational pull of dispensable weight.

When I was doing the first season of *The Apprentice*, I had limited knowledge of how shows work, how networks operate, and how shows are rated. Was this a problem? It could have been, but I saw it all as an opportunity to learn something new. I was the new kid on the block, and it could have been daunting, but I decided to go for it. It was like a crash course. Had I known that 95 percent of all new television shows fail, I might have thought twice about it. In that case, what I didn't know worked for me. I just put all my concentration into what I was doing, and as problems surfaced, I dealt with them. Think how boring it would be to just sail into things and have everything be perfect. You can't prove your merit on quiet waters, whether you're a businessman or a mariner.

Ralph Waldo Emerson wrote, "It is a lesson which all history teaches wise men, to put trust in ideas, not circumstances." That's a good way of saying you need to focus on your goals, not your problems. If people waited for everything to be perfect before attempting anything, the world would be in a sorry state. Maybe I just like challenges, but I have to say that without a challenge, I would find the world a little flat. Maybe that's one reason I like building skyscrapers.

As a builder, I know that being thorough when it comes to your problems will greatly reduce them. Being thorough means being meticulous. Don't toss off your problems, and don't dwell on them either. Deal with them! Who's the boss—your problems or you? Better make sure of your approach on that subject.

If Einstein turned his back on problems, I doubt if he'd be as quotable as he is today. He admits to staying with problems for a long time—an indication of his patience and perseverance. He thought about problems until he had them figured out. In other words, that's how he found solutions. That's a good way to go when it comes to just about anything. Maybe none of us are an Einstein, but we can learn from his approach.

If you've got some problems today, that's a good sign. It means you're alive for one thing. So give that some thought, and make the most of that situation.

Follow your bliss and the universe will open
doors where there were only walls.

—Joseph Campbell

Scotland:
You're Hired!

This story started two years ago and, as of November of 2008,
had a happy ending. I had spent five years reviewing sites
throughout Europe for a golf course and turned down over 200
possibilities for development. Then in 2006 I saw the links land at
Menie Estate, which is in northeast Scotland's Grampian Region.
I had never seen such a dramatic unspoiled seaside landscape—it
had three miles of spectacular oceanfront and sand dunes of immense proportions. To put it mildly, I was excited. I knew this was
the right place for my golf course, and I had two additional reasons
for that: My mother was born in Scotland, and Scotland is the birth-
place of golf.

This would be a labor of love for me, and I couldn't wait to
get started on my plans. Well, two years later, I can finally get
started. After I got full approval to go ahead, I realized this would
be a great business lesson for you to hear about. It's about determination and perseverance.

113

As soon as my proposed development was announced in 2006, environmentalists were immediately on guard. In fact, the environmental statement on this estate takes up two five-inch-thick books. Also, it would be an expensive development, costing one billion pounds. Anything I do means instant scrutiny, but the scope of my plans was such that no one thought I would get approval to go ahead. In short, there were a lot of issues to be dealt with, from badger and otter protection plans to the economic value to locals. I knew it wouldn't be easy. It became such a saga that the BBC filmed several documentaries and HBO did a feature on the project hosted by Bryant Gumbel. This was going to be a challenge, but there was no way I was going to give in or give up. When something matters, it matters.

People were expecting a duel, which I realized, so instead I offered a partnership approach. We worked with the Scottish National Heritage, and because we had the same concerns, it became clear that I am environmentally sensitive. I was also inclined to be sympathetic to the rich history of the area due to my own heritage, and I gave that aspect due respect. I also hired the leading expert on geomorphology (the study of movement landforms, such as sand dunes), and we did extensive research on the twenty-five acres of sand dunes on this land. I was thorough and painstaking, which I think was noticed.

The Scottish government held a public inquiry that lasted for five weeks, and my development had very broad local and business community support. The local politicians were for it, the environmentalists supported us, and a significant point is that the Scottish ministers also agreed with us. It turns out that it is one of the largest land-use applications approved in UK history. The locals were ecstatic, and considering the worldwide economy, I could understand that.

I could literally write a book about this development already, and we're just getting started. But I have to say this victory is particularly meaningful because it's been a victory for everyone. Scotland and the locals won, and so did I. We have received tremendous feedback from people who have watched this development over the past couple of years remarking on how tenacious we were to fight that long and that hard for it. There have been thousands of articles printed about it, and I received countless letters, mostly encouraging me to keep up the good fight. I'm known for being persistent, but this was and is truly a special case because it has to do with my roots. Apparently, those roots go very deep.

I made a point to visit my ancestral home (my mother's house on the Isle of Lewis) with my sister Maryanne during this time, which further cemented my determination. I think I surprised even the die-hards by the battle I fought and won. But it wasn't just business—it was personal, too. That can be a formidable combination.

In honor of my mother, Mary McLeod Trump, I kept the faith and won. She's the one who always told me, "Trust in God and be true to yourself." I'm glad I listened to her because that was very wise advice. Scotland has a true Scot behind them all the way, and Trump International Golf Links will soon grace the north coast of Scotland.

Tempo: the rate of motion or activity.

—WEBSTER'S DICTIONARY

~~~

Develop a Tempo When You're Working

I've mentioned before that when you're the CEO of a company, it's like being a general. You have to be in charge, you have to take responsibility, you have to instill confidence. But it's also a bit like being a conductor, which is one reason I mention tempo. Think about it: An orchestra is comprised of many parts, of many instruments and players, and when they all work well together, you will have an exceptionally good orchestra. But the conductor is the one responsible for the tempo, for the performance, for the teamwork—it's very much like having a well-run organization.

I operate quickly, which is allegro to an orchestra. My organization is the orchestra, but I'm the conductor. I'm very well aware of how important it is to keep the momentum going at all times, whether you're in the mood or not. My team will take the cue from me, and I know it. Learn to develop your own tempo and stick to it. See it as an inner metronome that keeps consistent time no matter what's going on around you.

People often ask me what makes me tick. I think that's part of it—I simply respond to my own tempo, and my mode is working fast. Maybe yours is slower, maybe it's even faster, but we all know what speed is best for us. Stick to that tempo and keep at it. People will learn to plug into that, and you will see faster results because of it. Can you imagine if every musician in the orchestra had their own idea of what the tempo should be? It'd be cacophony, a mess. That's what can destroy businesses, too. Be a good conductor and make sure you're all in accord on this basic component.

When I conduct a meeting, I'm in charge and I need people to keep up with me. People who work with me know my tempo, and they've adjusted. New people learn how. No matter what situation or business you are in, be alert to the level of energy around you—it will help you through every day. So if you're not in charge yet, realize it's your responsibility to take the cue and respond accordingly.

People talk about being in "the zone" when they reach a certain level of achievement, whether they are runners or writers. It's when things come naturally, a sort of synchronicity. I know the feeling when I am making deals and I see the pieces falling into place the way they should. It's something to aim for, and tempo has a lot to do with it.

For example, you probably all know the feeling of having to write a term paper. Sometimes it's not so easy to get started—maybe you've procrastinated, but finally one night you get down to it and, after awhile, you are producing the pages without a lot of agony. Thinking about doing it was probably harder than actually getting it done. Something takes over and the work evolves. A lot of that is tempo, or getting into the groove, and pretty soon performance takes over and you're done.

I've noticed that some people need a new speedometer because their positive momentum is so slow that they couldn't possibly expect to get anywhere. Their tempo is set at a big number in the minus category somewhere, and they still can't figure out why they haven't arrived anywhere yet. Some people may think they're born losers, but a tempo adjustment just might change that scenario.

There's another reason I like to use the word tempo. Tempo also refers to the game of chess; it's a turn to move in chess in relation to the number of moves required to gain an objective. Note that it refers to gaining an objective. We all know that chess is a game of strategy. So is business. Think about that—and develop a tempo starting today.

*No person who is enthusiastic about his work
has anything to fear from life.*

—Samuel Goldwyn

~⌒〜

You Can Better
Your Best
at Any Time

If you see every day as an important day for your future and a
special day just because you have it, you will be amazed at how
productive and energetic you will be. It's the best way to be at your
best at all times. Ever say to yourself, "what a great day!"? Say it
to yourself today, right now, and see how your enthusiasm level
begins to improve.

That's the first step, and it helps if you're already doing something you love doing. Things just work out better that way, and
you won't have to work very hard at creating momentum or enthusiasm. But no matter how well you've done, you can always do
more and do better. That's how I avoid complacency and how I
maintain a high level of productivity.

For example, after I'd finished Trump Tower and it became a
great success, I knew it was just the beginning, and I was right. I
kept moving forward and later built Trump World Tower at the

United Nations Plaza, which became another sensational success, critically and personally.

Maybe I thrive on challenges, but the most significant challenges are the ones you give to yourself. I don't need to impress anyone at this point, but I do need to satisfy my own goals and ideals. For example, The Trump Hotel Collection has taken The Trump Organization international in a short amount of time. It was a natural extension of our brand in the luxury sector of the hotel industry, and Donald Jr., Ivanka, and Eric have taken the concept worldwide. It has been exciting to see the growth and success of this collection, and it didn't happen because I was already satisfied with my achievements. I didn't put a limit on my own horizons.

Don't ever think you've done it all already or that you've done your best. That's just a shortcut to undermining your own potential. Unless you've already kicked the bucket, there's still a lot more you can do. We've all been around know-it-alls who remind me of the cynics who know the price of everything and the value of nothing. Avoid that trap by realizing your own potential and the intrinsic value of things, including your own efforts to make the day a great one for yourself—and others.

One task assignment on *The Apprentice* had the teams giving a techno expo for senior citizens. Part of the theme was to give back, so the assignment was given at Trump Place on the Hudson River, where I have donated a large park to the city of New York. As a reward, in keeping with our theme of giving back, the winning team went to a children's hospital to give presents and spend some time with the kids. Afterwards, the team members commented that while working with the seniors was a high, seeing the smiles on the children was the bonus. They'd been allowed to better their best effort, and their sincerity was obvious. Everyone had a great day. So do more, be more, give more—and everyone will benefit.

It is a curious fact that people are never so trivial
as when they take themselves seriously.

—OSCAR WILDE

They Thought I
Was Doing So Well

Soon after *The Apprentice* premiered and was a hit show, I became a popular choice for television commercials. I turned a
lot of them down, and I did a few, but one for Visa always remains
in my memory. It was funny and I was allowed to display a self-
deprecating attitude that I think took people by surprise. The surprising thing is that I'm more humble than people might think.
I'm humble enough to be grateful, for one thing, and I still have
a sense of humor about myself.

In this commercial, called "Rooftop," I am shown on top of
Trump Tower holding my Visa card when a gust of wind blows it
out of my hand and down many scores of floors to the street below,
which happens to be Fifth Avenue. Then I'm seen rummaging
through a Dumpster in search of my lost card, and when a well-
dressed passerby on Fifth Avenue sees me emerge from the bottom of the Dumpster, she indignantly remarks, "and I thought he
was doing so well!"

The idea of the ad was to show that I was learning about the security my Visa card could provide to me. The effect was that I'm a guy who would go through a Dumpster to make sure of it.

That sums up a lot about how I can be, which makes me a lot like everyone else, if you think about it. The part I like about some of the things I've done, when I look back, is that I'm not afraid to be seen as human, because I am. What would you do? What would I do? There's a lot we all have in common. Not that it was necessarily due to the protection the card offers—so the second lesson is that you should know what a product has to offer you to begin with. It could save you a visit to a Dumpster.

I remember being asked why I would appear on a popular national television show (*Saturday Night Live*) dressed in a pastel yellow suit in a skit called "Trump's House of Wings" accompanied by singing chickens. My answer is, "why not?" I will admit I nixed the idea of appearing in a chicken costume but the yellow suit I got in replacement wasn't exactly a step up. But it was a memorable skit and everyone had fun.

One number you didn't see on *Saturday Night Live* and one I liked a lot, as well, was about a romance novelist who was a real estate tycoon who lived in a skyscraper on Fifth Avenue. There were just too many skits and that one got cut. But I think I made a fine example of the possibilities of romance novels that can be based on fact. I have a great romantic streak and I live very happily and romantically in my Fifth Avenue apartment.

When I appeared on the Emmy Awards and sang the Green Acres theme with Megan Mullally, I know a lot of people were surprised, but we had fun. The same thing happened when I got into the ring and took a challenge from Vince McMahon of Wrestlemania. That was a stretch for a real estate developer, but it was definitely a new experience and one I enjoyed.

Here's my point: Don't be afraid of taking chances. Go for having a good time, because in the process a lot of other people just might have a good time, too. My theory is: Take your work seriously, take yourself less seriously. It's a great recipe for some good times and great memories.

Being good in business is the most fascinating
kind of art. Making money is art and working is art
and good business is the best art.

—ANDY WARHOL

~~~

It's Not
Personal—It's
Business

B usiness is about making money. It's about the bottom line. The sooner you realize that, the sooner you'll get a grasp about what business is. I'm very often surprised by people who think business is something else. They come in with lofty ideas and philanthropic purposes that have absolutely no place in a business meeting. It's a waste of everyone's time.

I remember when a group of businessmen wanted to build an atrium on the ground floor of 40 Wall Street. It was a beautiful idea. They wanted to make 40 Wall Street the downtown equivalent of Trump Tower, except they forgot about something. What would they do with the steel columns that support a seventy-two-story building? That rather major structural component never entered their minds. I hope they didn't take it personally when I pointed out their oversight.

Business is business. For example, if you get fired, there's usually a number behind it, and that can take the personal affront right out of it. Businesses have to watch out for their bottom line or they won't be in business for very long. Don't get worked up. If you do, you might be taking it the wrong way. It isn't always easy, but try to be objective.

I learned early on that business can be completely impersonal even when you're dealing with human beings. One banker I was dealing with was so indifferent that he was literally like a machine. When a machine says no, it's very tough. There's no negotiating possible. I remember writing that you'd be better off dealing with a killer with real passion than with an institutional type who has no emotion and just wanted to go home at 5 o'clock. Sometimes we run into brick walls like that. Our only recourse is to find another way around it, which I did. But I got a good insight into how impersonal business can be.

I'd rather be personable. It also works better, provides more options for everyone, and allows for more creativity. It can require more energy, but I can tell you the results will be worth it. It still strikes me as funny that I suddenly became very popular after I started firing people every week on national television. People really liked me for that. Or so I thought. What it was is that they were seeing the real person behind the famous name. They see that I can be tough but that I try to be impartial. I'm also a bit of a teacher. I've always been this way, but it was never seen before except by my employees. I'm personable, but I can be all business. Believe me, it's a formidable combination.

I have to be careful not to blow people away, because if you cross me personally and professionally, I'll have a double whammy waiting for you. I don't enjoy being vicious, but sometimes in self-defense it becomes necessary. I don't like the double standard, as in, whatever I do is okay and whatever you do isn't okay, or vice versa. If you treat me a certain way, then I can treat you that way, too. Some people call that the old "an eye for an eye" approach, but I call it playing fair. Sometimes the only way to deal with a bully is to punch him back. Let them know who they're dealing with. Fair play is fair play—and once again, don't take it personally.

It's wise to be circumspect, and some people just say "get yourself out of the picture" first in order to see the big picture. Don't take personally what is not meant personally. A lot of times people misdirect their anger, and if you take it personally, you'll become a punching bag for angry darts. I've had people say totally off-the-wall things to me, which I can now deflect, knowing that about 90 percent of the time their comments have next to nothing to do with me. You have to develop a thick skin, and keep your own positive wavelength going at all times.

Be tough, be smart, be personable, but don't take things personally. That's good business.

The important thing is not to stop questioning.
Curiosity has its own reason for existing.

—ALBERT EINSTEIN

Think Like
a Genius

E very morning I read a variety of newspapers, from local to national to international. This group includes the *Financial Times*
of the UK, the *New York Times*, the *New York Post*, the *Wall Street
Journal*, and more. Then I tune into the morning news programs
on television. By the time I get to the office, I have a good
overview of what's happening in the world. Considering what has
been happening lately, this kind of attention is absolutely necessary. It's also necessary for us to begin to think creatively.

I live and work in the same building, so I have a very short
commute and rarely run into traffic, and that is a tremendous time
saver. What I do is quickly assemble what I've just read about and
heard, and then I see how it pertains to any of the businesses I have
or deals I have in process. I also get updates throughout the day
on what is happening, both nationally and worldwide. There is no
way you can be effective without being informed, and this is more
important today than ever.

Control is about education. Lack of education or information can put you at bigger risk for losing control. Of course, there are things we can't control and there is an element of risk in our lives that we can't deny or overrule. But brain power equals a very powerful leverage. That doesn't equal being a know-it-all. I'm known as someone who asks a lot of questions. With the economic crisis causing major problems here and some big ripples around the globe, it seems some very informed yet creative thinking is in order.

Recently I read an article about some famed geniuses who included Aristotle, Leonardo da Vinci, and Einstein. Aristotle held metaphorical thinking in high esteem, Einstein found visualization to be helpful in solving problems, and da Vinci believed in restructuring a problem to make it more accessible or broader in scope. I realized that I did all of these things, but not necessarily deliberately.

All of them believed in chance. In fact, they prepared themselves for it and "creative accidents" would result, some of which have produced wonderful inventions. All of them kept an open mind and were full of a sense of wonder. I mention these components because each of them can be applied to business with some great results.

Sometimes people ask me how I do what I do. I don't always have an answer because part of the process is difficult to describe, but when I saw these points in the article, I realized that is definitely similar to what I go through to arrive at certain decisions. All of us have creative powers, so devote some time to learning about this process.

Someone asked me if I thought I was a genius. I decided to say yes. Why not? Try it out. Tell yourself that you are a genius. Right away you will probably wonder why and in what way you are a genius. And right away you will have opened your mind up to wonder—and to asking questions. That's a big first step to thinking like a genius, and it might unlock some of your hidden talents.

Another point made was that geniuses tend to produce. They are prolific. Not everything will be fantastic and mistakes will be made, but they have a huge volume of work to show for their brain power and their mastery of the thought process. Einstein mentioned that numbers and words had little to do with his thought process because he had learned to visualize. Yet he published hundreds of papers in the course of his career.

Another characteristic that geniuses tend to share is the ability to think in opposites. This is outside the boundaries of logic and allows your mind to operate on a new level. When it comes to business, this can be tremendously helpful as it's one way to see the ups and downs, the cycles, of finance and real estate, and know that as they happen, they can be dealt with.

Do not underestimate yourself, and know you are able to handle what comes your way. Just increase your leverage by learning to think like a genius. And remember Einstein's words: "Anyone who has never made a mistake has never tried anything new."

Great minds have purposes,
others have wishes.

—WASHINGTON IRVING

❧

Go Against the Tide

The world is rich with examples of originality. Original means independent and creative in thought and action. Nowadays we call it thinking outside the box, although the term supposedly derives from a puzzle created by an early-twentieth-century British mathematician. Whatever you call it, it very often means going against the tide, which may not be the easiest way to go. But sometimes the easiest way is also the mediocre way, and that's okay if that's your standard. But it isn't mine, and it most likely isn't yours either if you're taking the time to read this book.

When I was starting out in real estate, my father thought I was nuts to want to build in Manhattan. I was going against the tide, and I knew I was up against some pretty big odds, but I wanted to carve my own niche. I had my own ideas and knew I'd have to be independent as well as creative to see them happen. I'm certainly happy I decided to take the chance and to go for it. It would have been easier for me to just stay with the family business and leave it at that.

Fortunately, I had a good education and experience behind me. I always warn people not to jump into anything unprepared.

It's that old fine line between bravery and stupidity. Know the tides before you dive in. There's always a certain amount of danger, danger meaning the unknown, even in shallow waters. Riptides and sharks exist. Sometimes you don't see them until it's too late. Keep that in mind no matter how sensational or foolproof you think your idea might be.

Charles de Gaulle is a figure of historic importance, especially as it pertains to World War II, and he came from a family of historians and writers. In fact, his father taught literature and philosophy. But the young Charles de Gaulle had a passionate interest in military matters, and he was determined in every respect to pursue this unexpected passion. He was a force in world history known for his extraordinary stubbornness. He became known as "the man who said no" when he refused to accept the terms of the armistice with Nazi Germany. When he said no, he meant it. There was no equivocating. I don't know all the details of his early life, but I can imagine a boy from a family of intellectuals might have experienced some scrutiny when he displayed an intense interest in all things military. But he knew what he wanted to do, and he followed his own path.

It's a good idea to take your own pulse once in awhile instead of just focusing on what the masses are doing. Take a break from expectations, from the media, and plug into yourself. You might find that your electricity is better suited to another socket. You might have to exert yourself, but look at the alternatives that remain. Get out of your so-called comfort zone. I call it complacency, and it's a good way to get nowhere.

I remember firing someone who once said "I think it's good enough" when referring to project he was working on. Good enough? It wasn't good enough for me, and if it was good enough for him, he shouldn't be working for me. I want people who will go the extra mile to make it the best. Don't be so easily pleased—with yourself or with anything else. Be tough and keep your standards high, even if you have to fight the undertow.

We use the term "groundbreaking" in construction when a new building is about to begin construction. That term is also used to describe something that is new and creative, as in setting a new standard. Make your life as groundbreaking as possible, while also minding the tides and riptides around you. It's a good way to wind up on top.

Great works are performed not by
strength but by perseverance.

—SAMUEL JOHNSON

Think
Positively

There have been so many books and examples about the power of positive thinking that it seems unnecessary to even mention it. But I still see examples every single day of the power that negative thinking has over people, so either people haven't gotten the message or they're just plain not paying attention.

When I started thinking about this essay, I realized that maybe people just don't have the persistence required to make positive thinking work for them. Things rarely just happen overnight. Most overnight success stories are no such thing. Just because you only recently heard of someone doesn't mean they haven't been working for twenty or thirty years or more already. When my television show, *The Apprentice,* became a big hit, I had over thirty years of experience to draw upon when conducting the boardroom scenes. It wasn't just a fluke that I came across as someone who knew what they were doing. The fact that I was on television was new, but the rest wasn't particularly new to me. Business is business, whether it's being filmed or not. My business credentials and experience came into the picture as the necessary background for creating a show based on high-stake New York corporate business.

How does positive thinking fit into this *Apprentice* scenario? First of all, I didn't say no. I knew it was a risk, but I was positive about what might happen. If I'd chosen to listen solely to the negatives about the endeavor, such as "most new TV shows fail" or "reality TV is on the way out" or "you'll lose your credibility" or "you'll lose your grasp on your business empire" and about fifty other negatives, I never would have given it a thought. But instead, I chose a positive perspective. I asked myself the "what if" question. What if it was a success? What if I enjoyed it? What if it proved to be enlightening? What if it brought The Trump Organization the recognition it deserved? What if the jobs provided to the winners proved to be valuable stepping stones to deserving individuals? I had a long list of positives to go along with the negatives.

I'm a pragmatic positive thinker. When I hear people saying that anything you want to do is possible, that seems childish or at least uninformed to me. Some things are not going to happen. For example, if I suddenly decided tomorrow that I wanted to win a gold medal at the Olympics as a swimmer, and I was sure I could because I was so positive about it, well, I think I'd have to have some mental checks. It's not going to happen, no matter how hard I train. Or if I decided I was going to give Tiger Woods a run for his money as a golfer, starting tomorrow, I think I'd have to worry about being a little irrational. Be positive, but be realistic.

Back to the persistence issue. You have to be positive every single day. You have to put a daily effort into it, because believe me, no one else is going to help you with this. Most people think their lives will be easier if they have less competition. The fact that you believe in yourself could get in their way. Good. Get in their way!

Upset their status quo! Get out of your own static comfort zone by moving forward with the momentum and power that positive thinking and perseverance can give you. This takes energy, but the result will be stamina—positive stamina, a necessary ingredient for success.

Sometimes you just have to be tough. I use the example of a brick wall. Is there a brick wall getting in your way? Fine. That happens. But you have a choice. You can walk away from the wall. You can go over the wall. You can go under the wall. You can go around the wall. You can also obliterate the wall. In other words, don't let anything get in your way. Get a balance, and then let the positive outdistance the negative.

When I was building Trump National Golf Club in Briarcliff Manor, New York, I wanted to build a 110-foot waterfall. It pumps 5,000 gallons of water per minute and cost $7 million to complete. We moved granite and many tons of earth to achieve this spectacular effect, and if you think this happened easily and overnight, think again. But I was positive, I was persistent, and I refused to settle for anything less than what I had envisioned. The result was worth the effort, and not surprisingly, perseverance won. Keep that in mind in all your endeavors.

Men acquire a particular quality by
constantly acting in a particular way.

—Aristotle

~~~

People Have
Different Ways of
Achieving Results

We all have different ways of accomplishing things. Some people deliberate for a long time and then move quickly, some people make a quick decision and then take a long time getting around to doing something about it. Sometimes the results are exactly the same. The old saying "to each his own" is right because there is no right way or wrong way.

As an example, I like the story about a copywriter who would spend most of his time looking like he wasn't doing anything. He would gaze out the window for hours, sit doing nothing, and made no attempt to look busy. This drove his co-workers up the wall, so they finally complained to the boss. The boss became very interested in this report, asked them how long this behavior had been going on, and then told them all to see if they could get him coffee or lunch, anything to make sure his day wasn't interrupted. They became irate over this preferential treatment, so the boss told them, "The last time he acted like this, and the time before, and the time before, he came up with ideas worth millions of dollars. So whatever you do, don't disturb him!" You see—to each his own. We all have our own process. The results are what matter.

If someone wanted to review my work process, they might very easily say, "Well, he spends a lot of time on the telephone." That's true, I'm on the phone and talking a lot. But that's how I do a lot of business. It's not that I'm just chatting on the phone all day. It all depends on the way you want to see something or someone. You can color the situation or behavior in a favorable or unfavorable light. But bottom line, I get a lot accomplished. That's my style. If you want to say that all I do is have daily chat fests and still manage to rake in the big bucks, that's fine with me. My achievements still point toward effectiveness.

Find the most productive way of working for yourself. I don't mind working hard, but I see no merit in working stupidly. Looking like you're working hard is a waste of everyone's time and talent. What's the best way to accomplish your goals for that day? Some people work very hard for several hours and accomplish more than other people do in two days. It's all a matter of focus.

After awhile, people will know you by your habits—or your habitual behavior. These habits can be qualities, as Aristotle points out. If your behavior is consistently of a high standard, your particular quality may be integrity. That's a good way to go. So review your habits and make sure they are leading you in the right direction. In other words, make sure you are working toward the results you want to see, and know that your way of achieving them will be distinctly your way. It's also a great way to define your own boundaries without being influenced negatively by anyone else.

As a young man, I remember when someone once told me that the clearest way to see people and events was to be nonjudgmental—to just see and record the facts without coloring them with "this is right" or "this is wrong" or telegraphing the desired reaction to other people. It's a journalistic approach—journalism in its purest sense—that allows the decision to be made entirely by the individual. In other words, news without a slant. It requires a little more thinking, but sometimes I think we need to do a little bit more of that these days.

We should never think our way is the only way, whether we're talking about work ethics or politics. We should be grateful for the diversity we have in our lives and take the time to hone our own natural talents. Sometimes we don't know how long or how hard someone has worked to achieve something. Warren Buffet has a fortune worth many billions of dollars now, but he started out selling chewing gum when he was six years old. He made two cents a pack.

Results are what matter. The bottom line is clearly the bottom line. It's not always a straight line to achieving the results we are looking for, but rather a series of efforts that will add up to experience and achievement. Look at how many years scientists will work toward a discovery and you will understand how patience is one of the ingredients for success. So set your pattern now for achievement of the highest quality. That's your task assignment for the long term.

Do not go where the path may lead,
go instead where there is no path
and leave a trail.

—RALPH WALDO EMERSON

~⌐

Discover and
Live Your Purpose

One thing I've learned about life is that it is a series of discoveries. It starts with discoveries and hopefully should continue that way. Remember how exciting it was to learn to ride a bike? Ever watched a child taking their first steps? It's a momentous occasion. If we can capture that kind of excitement every day, I think we're on our way to wisdom.

Albert Einstein said, "The mind that opens to a new idea never comes back to its original size." I agree. Once you've learned to walk, why would you want to go back to crawling around? It wouldn't make sense. We all have a purpose in life, and that's to do our best to live up to our potential.

It's really pretty simple. All we have to do is tune in to our talents and capabilities. Remember, I didn't say it was easy—I said it was simple. Sometimes we get so distracted that it's hard to tune out enough to be able to tune in at all. We are bombarded by outside information all day. The challenge here is to find the quiet time to be able to assimilate our own inside information in the midst of all the cacophony. You have to unplug before you can plug yourself back in.

I'm a busy guy, but I set aside quiet time every morning and every evening to keep my equilibrium as it should be—which is centered on my own path. I don't like being swayed by anything that might be negative or damaging. When Emerson talks about leaving a trail, he's right. That means you can't be following someone else's path. That means you'd better spend some time focusing yourself on your own path and your own purpose.

This is a serious issue, for worldly as well as personal reasons. The worst things in history have happened when people stop thinking for themselves and listen to other people and, even worse, start following other people. That's what gives rise to dictators. Avoid that at all costs. Stop it first on a personal level and you will have contributed to world sanity as well as your own.

In business, I've discovered that my purpose is to do my best, to my utmost ability, every day. That's my standard. I learned early in my life that I had high standards. Ever hear of intrinsic value? Intrinsic means basic, inborn, elemental. If you have an intrinsic value, it cannot be taken away or shaken. It's a form of strength that can be unbeatable.

Discovery means finding out something we didn't previously know. Purpose is an intention or an end to be attained. We have the tangible and the intangible in life. Let them balance each other out to your best advantage. I may be in a reality-based business, but I have a sense of the mystery in life that keeps me feeling like an explorer. Don't put blinders or borders on yourself.

I could have very easily dismissed Mark Burnett's idea for *The Apprentice* simply based on the fact that I was already very busy. But it was a new challenge and a new discovery for me. It served a part of my nature, which is that of an educator. Finding your purpose may be a lifelong pursuit or you may have found it when you were five years old. There's no absolute timeline for anyone. That's a good reason to never give up, to keep on discovering things every day. It's also a terrific recipe for a successful life. Following your own path will bring you to the places you were meant to be. Expand your horizons! In other words, think big and live large.

Freedom is not the right to live as we please,
but the right to find how we ought to live
in order to fulfill our potential.

—RALPH WALDO EMERSON

∽

Set the Standard

People who work for me know that my media persona of being positive and enthusiastic isn't just a façade. I am that way—from the inside out. I have big ideas and a big enough energy resource to get them done. Those who are around me will eventually catch on that that is how I operate. It's an effective approach that obviously works. It's contagious in the best sense of the word. One thing everyone knows about The Trump Organization is that we get things done and our energy level is one reason why. I've set the standard and everyone follows suit.

If you like to work hard, you will attract people with the same ethic. The people who work with me enjoy the daily challenges and set their own standards to meet those challenges. Their pattern of thinking matches mine—how do we accomplish more? How do we get to where we want to go? It's a combination of vision, courage, and discipline to realize that the possibilities are always there. But if you're thinking too small, you might miss them. Learn to think big.

Ask yourself this question: What standard would you like to be known for? Then go about setting that standard for yourself. No one else can set it for you. I can remember when my father couldn't understand why I wanted to develop in Manhattan. I'd had my eye on Manhattan since I was in college, and it was a goal I intended to reach. Years later, when I was describing my ideas for Trump Tower to my father, including the glass and bronze exterior, he couldn't understand why I would choose anything other than bricks to build with. Bricks worked for him, so why not for me? Because I was setting my own standard. When Trump Tower opened to wonderful reviews and became a landmark building, it was clear that my standard had been accepted—and in a big way.

I had also been advised to put up beautiful paintings in the lobby of Trump Tower. To me, this seemed old-fashioned and un-original, even though I like beautiful art. I decided to put up a waterfall, which to me is like a sculpture in itself, and it has attracted far more attention than if I'd put up paintings. It's over eighty feet high and cost $2 million to build. It's absolutely spectacular and I've never regretted my choice. Once again I was setting my own standard.

When I decided to rebuild Wollman Rink in Central Park, I did so with my own ethics in mind. Do the best job as quickly as possible for the least amount of money. The city had been trying for seven years to rebuild and restore this beautiful skating rink, and I finally interceded and finished it in three months and at less than 10 percent of the City's $21 million cost. Everyone benefited. Those are my standards, and I met them. I have my father's four-step formula to thank for my economy when doing a job: Get in, get it done, get it done right, and get out.

A question I would ask you to ask yourself to give you a jump start in thinking big is this: What is your creative capital? What do you have to offer? What have you acquired in your experience and in your studies that makes you valuable? Are you aware of your own potential? Will you be equipped to make a difference when the time comes for you to step forward? Start thinking along those lines and your worth will have already been multiplied.

A few years ago, probably in 2005, I received a phone call from Coach Mike Leach (who was fired unfairly from Texas Tech in December 2009), calling to say how much he liked my books because they were inspirational. I follow college football, so I knew he was the coach for Texas Tech, and a great one. We had a conversation and I realized we shared a few things in common as far as motivation and positive focus go. Since then I've appeared on ESPN for his team and he's appeared on *60 Minutes.* I mention him because there are some good reasons why Coach Leach is in the big leagues as far as great coaches go—he knows how to get the best from his players, he has an open mind, and he knows that being a coach means being able to teach others to think in new directions. That means their performance will be altered as well. Coach Leach knows what he's doing and how to do it, and he recognizes and develops the potential in other people. He's a great guy in addition to being a success.

Maybe you don't have a coach in your life, but if you set your own standards, acknowledge your own value, and remain positive from the inside out, you will be heading in the right direction for a very promising future.

*Intuition is perception
via the unconscious.*

—Carl Jung

◦◦◦

Go with Your Gut

We've all heard of instincts, intuition, and perception. In fact, all of us have these things. The important thing is to know how to use them. You may have superb academic credentials, but without using your instincts you might have a hard time getting to—and staying at—the top.

This is one of those gray areas that remain an enigma even to those who have finely honed business skills. It's hard to pin down or to explain how business instincts are acquired. Some of them are inexplicable. But there are signs that can guide you to or away from certain deals and certain people.

For example, within a few seconds of meeting Mark Burnett, the creator of *The Apprentice,* I knew he was 100 percent solid, both as a person and as a professional. On the other hand, I've met people that I have an aversion to for no particular reason, and while I try not to be judgmental, I have reason by now to trust my gut. Carl Jung said our conscious minds use only 5 percent of our brain power for daily functioning. If we can learn to tap into that unconscious, subconscious, and dormant 95 percent, the results can be amazing. Sometimes I think that's what helps our perceptive abilities come to our aid.

It's also a matter of tuning in. Ever notice how when we are in a situation that produces heightened alertness, whether it's a survival course or trying to pass an important exam, how careful we are in our responses? Suddenly, everything we say or do matters a lot. That's one way to notice how our instincts are there for us. Logic may say one thing, instincts may say another. Ideally, you should hone the best of both to make the best decisions.

I remember when I was acquiring 40 Wall Street, and literally every person I met with recommended that it be turned into residential units. I didn't agree. My gut instincts told me it was a great business location. I remained steadfast in my beliefs and the building now houses businesses that are thriving. It's been a lucrative deal for everyone, and 40 Wall Street is now worth in excess of $500 million.

When I was first starting out with my golf courses, my instincts told me it was a good direction to go. Logically, I knew that I had a passion for golf already, which is a crucial element for success, and that if I combined that with knowledge of the process, I'd have my bases covered. I found the best golf course designers in the world and spent many hours working with them. The results have been tremendous. I paired both instinct and logic to get these results.

Just as you would weigh your decisions carefully, be alert to your instincts and what they are trying to tell you. Spend some time with this innate aspect of yourself. See handling your instincts as an acquired skill—they can give you an edge in many situations, business or otherwise. There are a lot of things we can't see or hear, and our instincts are there to guide us. For example, if you were in the jungle, which would you prefer, a map or a guide? I know I'd feel more comfortable with a guide. A guide has experience and is right there beside you. Your instincts are within you, so use them accordingly.

Be sincere; be brief; be seated.

—FRANKLIN D. ROOSEVELT

~~~

Know Your Audience

A big key to winning is knowing where the other side is coming from. Whether you are involved in negotiations, a war, or in public speaking, this information can be invaluable. It's also necessary if you hope to connect in any way with other people. And in keeping with FDR's public speaking advice, getting to the point is greatly appreciated by everyone.

A great portion of life and business involves acting. Life *is* a performance art, no matter what field you are in. I've come to understand that fact over the years, and it's a helpful thing to realize. It includes people skills, negotiation skills, public relations, salesmanship, and the ability to read your audience, whether that audience is four people in your office or forty thousand at a speech. The same technique applies.

First of all, consider this: Is there a common denominator between you? Sometimes, even the weather can be a good starting point. Inclement or severe weather can affect all of us, whether we are billionaires or college students. That's an obvious one. Others take more time to determine. I can remember negotiating with someone I didn't like very much, which put up an invisible wall between us, until I discovered he was an avid golfer like myself. We suddenly had something to talk about that we both enjoyed, and proceedings went better after that.

I've heard many stories of how people end up with terrific jobs, not because of their college grades, but because of their hobbies and endeavors outside of their field. Granted, they had the credentials, but so do a lot of people. The people in charge of hiring were looking for something else, something extra—a common denominator aside from the obvious requirements. I know a young lawyer who was hired by a top law firm because in addition to doing well in law school, he also had a master's degree in music. This mattered because the partner doing the hiring happened to be a musicologist in his private time, and he was aware of the amount of discipline a degree in music requires. But it would also provide them with a mutual interest outside the usual legal environment that would enhance their daily routine.

Comedians know how to plug into their audience. The best public speakers know how to do that, too. Step number one is to know who your audience is. In my book *How to Get Rich,* I mention the common denominator as a way to relate to people. Ask yourself, what do we all have in common? I may be a billionaire, but I get stuck in traffic jams, too. I have bad days just like everyone else. Realize that a lot of your experiences can be understood and appreciated by your audience because they've had them, too. Make an effort to find what you have in common and lead with it. You will create a bond that didn't exist before if you will take the time to think about it.

I recently spoke to an audience of about 40,000 people. Afterwards, a member of my staff asked me if I ever got nervous. I said that I had finally realized that a large part of life was acting, and public speaking was just a part of that. I also thought about the people who would be in the audience instead of my own performance. That perspective frees you up from nervousness to allow you to focus on and know your audience.

Save yourself from some unnecessary learning experiences and realize that life is a performance art. Understand that as a performer, you have a responsibility to your audience to perform to the best of your ability. You also have to have the goods to hold your audience, no matter what the size may be. Performers prepare for every performance. That's showmanship, and that's life. Prepare yourself every day. Learn, know, and show. It's a proven formula. Put it to use starting today.

2009 will not be the Endless Summer—
but it may be the beginning of Spring.

—Thomas J. Barrack, Jr.

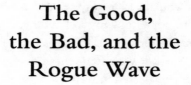

The Good,
the Bad, and the
Rogue Wave

My friend Tom Barrack of Colony Capital is a brilliant guy, and he sent me an article he wrote in late November of 2008 with the headline: "Today's Debt is Equity *Plus* a Few Suggestions to Help President-Elect Obama Ease the Pain." He bullet-pointed the latest events pertaining to the economy—twenty-two of them—and I realized that at any other time, just a few of these would be huge topics in themselves. It's a good indication of how alert we need to be.

His CliffsNotes summary: "Real estate is experiencing a seismic liquidity shock as a result of a complete closure of the credit and capital markets for both debt and equity. CRE (commercial real estate) and the debt which fueled its growth are in a massive meltdown."

Then he adds: "And just when we thought that all of the unpredictables had passed—a tribe of African pirates in speed boats hijack a Saudi tanker for ransom—a satirical headline read: 'Somali Pirates in Discussions to Acquire Citigroup.'"

All this and pirates, too. Somehow it helps to know the world hasn't changed all that much if pirates are still out there doing their thing. That's one take on it. The other take is that vigilance is certainly necessary in every walk or strait of life—which brings me to the topic of Bernard Madoff and his scheme that came to our attention in December of 2008.

I can remember when Bernard Madoff would approach me in Palm Beach, Florida, about investing some money with him. He'd say "Why don't you invest in my fund?" I didn't know much about him and I'm not a fund guy so I said no. I had enough going on in my own businesses that I didn't need to be associated or involved with his. Madoff was a frequent visitor at my Mar-a-Lago Club, and he was a respected guy.

I know people who have been victims of his unscrupulous scheme and what's happened to them is dreadful. He is without a doubt a sleazebag and a scoundrel without par. The sad thing is that so many people trusted him and unfortunately some of them trusted him completely. Some people gave 100 percent of their money to this guy, and now they're literally selling their houses in order to live. It's a great lesson in doing your due diligence. Some very smart people were taken in by him. Just because someone is well established doesn't mean they're not above being a total crook. He was a Svengali for rich people and he could wipe out hundreds of millions of dollars after just one phone call.

Even the people in his own organization supposedly didn't know about it, nor did his sons, he claims. He had several floors in a major office building. How could one man be manipulating that much money without at least some of the people knowing about it? The word here is greed. He certainly "made off" with some big bucks.

I know people are stunned by their losses and rightly so. I think we would all do well to pay heed to all of our transactions no matter how much we might respect or like someone. But the main lesson is never to invest 100 percent of your money with one person or in one entity. Even if someone or something is great, you can't bet the ranch on it, especially a person—they can become dishonest or they can become sick. In Madoff's case I think it was a combination of both. But you've got to spread your money around with numerous people, or at least three or four. You can't have your well-being determined by one person. My CliffsNotes summary: There are no guarantees but there are precautions. Do not let your guard down. Focus on the positives—but don't forget about the pirates.

The Rogue Wave

In January, Tom Barrack sent me his notes for a 2009 Survival Kit. I am sharing them with you because he tells a great story and he has an equally great insight in applying it to what's been going on. Included here are the first two pages of his four page essay, and I hope everyone will give this their full attention:

> The constant turmoil of the recent market is reminiscent of a story Laird Hamilton shared with us at our last annual meeting. No one has mastered the art of living more than Laird. He has spent his life in preparation and anticipation of riding big waves. The biggest waves in the Hawaiian Islands occur on Maui at a surf spot named Jaws. These waves reach 50 to 70 feet and can only be ridden by a few daring professionals utilizing "tow in surfing." Tow in surfing was invented to "turbo charge" the entry speed of a surfer to match the speed of the mountainous walls of fury which would otherwise be unconquerable by traditional paddling

techniques. Tow in will take you deeper and faster and allow you to ride waves that were unthinkable. A little bit like leveraged loans and derivatives in leveraged buy out land.

One morning Laird and one of his surfing mates, Brock Lickle, were in search of bigger waves and less surfers. They pulled around the corner from Jaws to a spot near the Maui airport which was virgin territory and breaking at 60 to 100 feet wave heights. They watched, analyzed and thought these just might be the waves of the decade. Even though there was no one else in the water they started to sea, racing up the huge wave faces and pounding through white water trying to get through the treacherous break. Just as they thought they had made it through the impact zone they looked to the horizon and saw a rogue wave roaring towards shore. They raced as hard as they could towards its looming face, but couldn't climb it in time and were tossed like rag dolls to the depths of the dangerous coral reefs. Laird related that he was no longer afraid at these moments because he had been in so many fearful situations in his decades of preparation that this was now his comfort zone. Both were the best in the world and knew that survival depended upon a few basic elements:

~ Remain calm—don't panic

~ Save your "dry powder" (air)

~ Don't fight the current—let it have its way with you

~ Don't question your ability to survive—know that you have trained and prepared a lifetime for this moment

~ Remember when you get to the top, the another wave will no doubt pound you again

~ Monitor all conditions—sight, sound, smell, motion, pressure

~ Stabilize your own situation then look out for your buddy

~ Once you find your buddy, survival will depend on both of you sharing the pain

Laird and Brock had to hold their breath for up to four minutes as they dove to the bottom trying to avoid their limbs being ripped apart by the ferocious impact as wave after wave kept coming at them. Finally, Laird made it to the top of the last wave of the set and anxiously searched for his buddy. He saw Brock floating 200 yards away in a pool of blood and no jet ski. He swam through the washing machine to Brock to find him badly injured and bleeding. Before Laird could get them both to shore he had to take off his wetsuit and, in MacGyver-like fashion, use it as a tourniquet on his buddy's nearly severed leg. He then wrapped his arms around Brock and swam them both to the jet ski bobbing in the crashing surf. He threw Brock on top and opened throttle to shore. Of course, the shore break was 30 feet high so the landing on the beach was the next heroic act. Laird picked his spot, gunned the jet ski, flew over the top of the wave and landed in the parking lot, which was now filled with hundreds of spectators. Laird pulled Brock off the jet ski to safety and then standing on shore realized that he was stark naked.

Once Brock was turned over to the emergency team and it was established that he would be okay, Laird grabbed another teammate and a new jet ski and marched back out into the monumental surf. He was not fearful. He got back on the horse (or jet ski in this case) and caught some of the best waves of his life. By taking the worst wipeout of his life he was now better equipped than those other professionals who had been watching unscathed from the parking lot.

HUMBLING 2008

2008 has been a year filled with surprises, volatility, disappointment, unfulfilled expectations and cyclic shock waves. As a new year dawns, I think it is important that we take a deep breath, relax and focus on the ingredients that are key to our continued survival. We must get back on the horse.

My boys share Laird's love of surfing and in order to convince them to spend time with Dad, it requires Christmas vacations that involve waves. Being in the ocean watching the never-ending changes in the sea allows me to reflect on the similarity of the survival tools needed in these chaotic times.

The first great lesson is that of humility. No matter how good you are, when arrogance raises its ugly head, Mother Nature will put you back into your box. Mastery of a wave involves being attuned to all the circumstances surrounding you. It is not about domination—it is actually about submission. The currents, the riptides, the swell, the wind, the reefs, the temperature, the crowds, the shapes are changing every second. The quest, then, is not to stabilize the wave and make each one exactly alike and predictable by all, but rather to perfect your own adaptability to an ever-changing situation and make it through to the other end. If you can survive, great. If you have executed it with style and grace, even better. In this quest, wipeouts are a way of life and planning to never be wiped out is foolhardy at best. World-class surfers train endlessly to be able to handle the inevitable trip to the "dark room." It involves preparation, anticipation, calmness and an ability to control one's fear. It is knowing **what** to do when everything goes wrong and you are gasping for breath. What surfers call "dry drowning"—to panic, flail and waste your valuable breath—is the worst thing you can do, even though it is the most intuitive. Experienced surfers concentrate on relaxing and not fighting the bone-crushing power of the wave until it relinquishes its force. They must be able to preserve their "dry powder"—to hold their breath and avoid being smashed on the coral reefs beneath them. This confidence comes from experience in previous wipeouts and a knowledge that they are truly prepared for the worst.

Furthermore, one surfer's wipeout is another surfer's "wave of the day." It is all about anticipation and being in the right position, which is not necessarily the position that the rest of the surfers are seeking. Not following the crowds can be the difference between victory and defeat. At the same, time one must watch the crowd and where it's going as their amateur moves can cause more damage than the wave alone.

The great surfers do not throw away their trained "tool kit" to harness differing wave conditions. They adapt to the circumstances which they are dealt. Their commitment and dedication are steadfast. They will wait for their spot and pay attention to everyone and everything around them using all of their senses. Those senses are defined and refined by instincts born from repetition—riding thousands and thousands of previous waves in all conditions. They will first concentrate on surviving, then positioning, then dominating the next wave.

Investing at this moment feels exactly the same. The sea is swirling, the currents are crossed, the swells are ebbing and flowing, the novices are drowning and there is grand wipeout after grand wipeout of some of the great names, which is intimidating and daunting to all.

Now is *that* moment for investing. **Now** is *that* moment when private equity has its greatest opportunity and its greatest challenge. The turbulence we have experienced in 2008 will dictate the circumstances for new investments, which will surely find historically high returns. History has shown that private equity returns soar at these deep inflection points in stabilized markets. Following the downturns in the early '90s and 2000s, returns were upwards of 25% for US private equity firms.

My thanks to Tom Barrack for his consistently great insights. Let's all remember to be champions in every situation and in all conditions—starting right now.

Building Your
Reputation

I've been building the Trump brand for several decades, and my
three eldest children are now with The Trump Organization,
helping to expand our brand. Don Jr., Ivanka, and Eric are all here
now. They are my real Apprentices, and they're doing a great job.
They know that I'm demanding, but they are disciplined and very
hard workers, so they are a good fit with The Trump Organization.

Having a quality brand is very much like having a good reputation. It's important to consider that fact, even when you are
just starting out. Remember that everything you say and do is important. Actions matter. You are, literally, your own brand, whether
you have a business yet or not. If you are serious about what you're
doing, taking responsibility for yourself starts now.

The Trump brand has to represent the highest quality available, no matter what the enterprise might be. If I build a golf
course, it has to the best. If I build a skyscraper, it has to be the
best. If I have a line of suits, they'd better be terrific. I am very

169

thorough when it comes to certain things. Namely, *everything.* You'd better be, too, if you hope to get somewhere worth going.

I remember when someone mentioned how impressed they were that I would be so interested in trees when I was building a golf course. I had made an effort to find the leading expert of this particular type of tree and spent a lot of time researching them on my own. But I was surprised they were impressed—to me it made sense. You have to know the details yourself! Secondhand information will always be secondhand. Don't be a secondhand person. Go to the source yourself. That's a start on the road to a great brand, a great reputation, or both. No detail is too small, whether it's a tree or a faucet. One assistant remembers that I kept three bathroom sinks on a couch in the office for months, asking everyone who came in which sink they liked best. To me, that kind of attention is a component of a comprehensive level of excellence.

Some of my buildings have sold out before they are built. Why? People recognize the brand name and know what they will be getting—the best for their money. It's not a risk on their part. That's the great thing about building a business based on quality and integrity. It will sell itself. It doesn't happen overnight—you may have to work awhile to establish your reputation and brand— but the consistency will be the standard to beat in your chosen industry. I can tell you, it's worth it. Whatever your interests are, get started. As Henry Ford said, you can't build a reputation (or a brand) on what you are *going* to do. You have to put some action into your plans, ideas, and dreams.

Most of us need letters of recommendation now and then. I write them as well as receive them, and I always look for the words "responsible, professional, and loyal." If you can build your reputation on three words, those would be three at the top to choose from. I also think of those words when it comes to the Trump brand—to be authentic when it comes to responsibility, professionalism, and loyalty—to my buyers, clients, students, readers, audiences, and so forth. I'll be the first to admit it's not always easy. I am responsible for a lot of people. But high standards are high standards, and that's what I stand for. I will not accept less from myself.

To build the reputation you want to have, you will have to be the same way. Being stubborn has its rewards. Getting to the top and staying there is one of them. Start now, start today, start this very minute. There's a lot of competition out there, and they won't be waiting around for you.

Build your reputation on intelligence, responsibility, and results. That's building the right way.

Diligence is the mother of good luck.

—BENJAMIN FRANKLIN

~~⌒⌒

"The Harder I Work, the Luckier I Get"

I've always been big on quotes, whether they're mine or someone else's, because very often they distill ideas down to their essence. What Ben Franklin said many years ago could have been said today, because it's relevant and right on. We've all heard about doing our "due diligence," which is another way of being thorough. It's also the first step to bringing yourself some good luck. What Gary Player, the great golfer, said—quoted above as the title of this essay—remains solid nutshell advice that can apply to everyone.

The mixed-use concept of hotel and condominiums has been a huge success, starting with the first one I did in New York City in the late 1990s, Trump International Hotel & Tower at 1 Central Park West. Since then I've built hotel towers in Chicago and Las Vegas, with many more in the works around the world. Our tower in Waikiki was sold out in five hours, which is a record. People ask me, "How can you do so much?" and I have to say it really isn't luck, but doing due diligence and applying common sense.

This mixed-use concept was obviously a winner, so I developed the idea further and then took it worldwide. The strategy has worked, and we now have a Trump Hotel Collection that encompasses the world. I had always known the Trump brand would go global—at the right time.

You can apply that to your own life, career, and business as well. Look into the future a bit. Take the time to move yourself forward. If the indications are there, put in the extra effort to make something good even better, or bigger, or both. That's thinking big, and I'm no stranger to that concept and you shouldn't be either. I've had enough success to know that it works.

The past few years of my life have been busier than they've ever been. Everything has escalated, and it's been demanding— but exciting. But I've also been preparing for it for a long time. I'm used to working hard, and therefore I'm used to expecting results. Some people call it luck, but like Ben Franklin said, diligence has something to do with it, too.

For example, if you've been working toward something for five years, I'd say you have a goal in mind. You've probably focused on that goal. Hopefully, you've been diligent in pursuing it. If your work pays off, which it most likely will, people might say you're just lucky. Maybe so, because you're lucky enough to have the brains to work hard!

When I'm writing a book, which seems to be most of the time these days, I will spend up to seven or eight months putting together notes, collecting articles, dictating stories and ideas before I even begin to actually put it all together. It's a long process, and it requires patience and perseverance to see it through to the finished product. I will admit that sometimes I wonder if it's worth it, because it's not an easy endeavor. But when the book is done, it's a great feeling. It's an accomplishment that has taken painstaking time. People won't see the work that goes into a book, but anyone who has written one will tell you that diligence is a must. They don't just materialize out of nowhere.

Recently, while working on one of my books, I spent some time thinking about the "entitlement mentality" that seems to have afflicted this country. I think we can take it back a few decades to the emergence of what was called "instant gratification" as personified by the superstars and rock stars who emerged and made tremendous amounts of money, which very much impressed young people. Suddenly, everyone thought they should have what those very few people had or that those people were "overnight" stars and it should happen that way to them, too. In reality, it happens to very few people and rarely does it happen "overnight" to anybody. Those are the exceptions to the rule, not the norm. But they received so much media attention that people who had to struggle a bit or work for long years at something had the feeling they were being left out or that they were being treated unequally. They began to feel that the world owed them something.

Not everything works out as we might hope it will, and certain fields require a bigger dose of luck to succeed in than others, but a very good way to pave your own way to success is simply to work hard, to be diligent, and to look at what you have going for you versus what you *don't* have going for you—the old cup half full versus half empty test. Here's where I bring back my tried and true theory that you have to think big—because if you're diminishing your own prospects, then it's not likely you will run into a lot of luck. And part of doing your due diligence is to know what *you* want for yourself, not what other people want for you—which in many cases turns out to be not much! Take the time to move *yourself* forward. In other words, think, work—and be lucky.

Empty pockets never held anyone back.
Only empty heads and empty
hearts can do that.

—Norman Vincent Peale

How to Get Rich

I wrote a book that came out in 2004 called *How to Get Rich*. I can remember when I was discussing appropriate titles with the editor, and we had a list of them. We kept going back and forth with different ideas, with clever and catchy titles. I finally said, "What everyone wants to know is how to get rich. Why don't we just call the book *How to Get Rich*?" To me, that was getting to the point. I'd appreciate that as a reader, so that's the title we chose.

Getting rich isn't always simple. I have and will always continue to emphasize the importance of loving what you do first. If your goal is just to make money, you are shortchanging yourself. You might also run out of energy while you're trying to make that money. Passion is an incredible source of fuel that can get you through the tough spells that are bound to come up. So the first step in preparing to becoming rich is to find something that you absolutely love doing.

Maybe you don't know what you want to do yet. That's fine—just set your compass to finding out what it is, and there's a good chance you'll discover it. Meantime, learn everything you can about as many subjects and businesses as you possibly can. Knowledge is never a waste of time. I had studied the entertainment business a bit when I was younger, even though I had decided to go into real estate, and sure enough I ended up being in the entertainment business later in life. That was not wasted time, even though I hadn't consciously planned to enter that field. Now I have a production company in Los Angeles, Trump Productions, and we're entering the eighth season of *The Apprentice*. Considering that the first *Apprentice* season started in January of 2004, NBC, Mark Burnett, and I have had a very successful time of it.

It's important for you to know something about this story. I didn't do *The Apprentice* for money. That was not my incentive. I was initially paid next to nothing. Happily, it became a hit show, and the result is that it gave publicity to my brand, which has garnered greater financial success for me than ever before.

Sometimes being too cautious is the greatest risk of all. Preparation and organization will help to downsize the element of risk that is often involved in becoming rich. If you are well prepared and have everything in order, you will have provided yourself with a safety net. The best way to do that is to learn to be highly efficient. Highly efficient people keep their bases covered. Easier said than done, but it's a skill set that you can acquire for yourself.

Efficiency is the productive use of time. Learn to monitor yourself and the amount of time you use to focus on any specific thing. Having a time limit can be a terrific way to make your brain work at its most effective pace. I remember reading about an order of monks who have a determined amount of time for each duty, then a bell rings and they stop and immediately go on to their next chore. Creating and employing a discipline of focus is a good way to avoid spending more time than necessary on any one thing. I had an editor who, after a meeting with me in my office, commented that he needed oxygen. He wasn't accustomed to the fast pace he encountered, and I think he learned something about economy of time.

In summing up, if you want to get rich, two important considerations are passion and efficiency: Have passion for what you do and be efficient about it at the same time. That combination has worked for me.

*Individual commitment to a group
effort—that is what makes a team work.*

—Vincent Lombardi

Work with
People You Like

There's a saying I remember that is appropriate for this subject: "If you're going to live in the river, better make friends with the crocodiles." That being said, let's proceed to this topic, which hopefully will help to make your business life as reptile-free as possible.

I've been fortunate to work with people I like. Some of my employees have been with me for twenty, twenty-five, even thirty years. If we didn't like each other, that would be a long-term sentence of misery. As it is, we work together well, we respect each other, and we get a lot accomplished. Management becomes a whole lot easier if you are careful when finding employees or partners.

People I work well with have to work fast. That's how I work, and they follow suit. Allen Weisselberg, my CFO, Rhona Graff, VP and my chief assistant, and Jeffrey McConney, my controller, have the ability to distill a lot of information and can explain something to me with a minimum of words, sometimes ten words or less. Considering how much I have to do every day, I appreciate this brevity. George Ross, Senior Counsel, Jason Greenblat, General Counsel, and Matthew Calamari, my COO, have the same ability. It's not that I don't enjoy talking with them on a personal level, but our agendas have to be attended to and by now we all know how to get things done quickly, both individually and as a team. The respect goes both ways, and it's a great environment for everyone.

If you can get a core group around you that you like and who understands your needs, you will be heading in the right direction. Sometimes I think it's divine intervention when the right people show up, because as we all know, it happens that people who give great interviews sometimes aren't so great, and vice versa. In that sense, every hire is a bit of a gamble. Solid gold credentials don't always mean solid gold people, but sometimes they do. You have to give people a chance to prove themselves. But in the interim, it helps a lot if you like having them around to begin with.

You will have to see beyond what is presented to you. Every person has unique talents that may or may not be in their job description or listed on their resume. People are not one-dimensional. I don't like being underestimated or stereotyped, so it is safe for me to assume that other people don't like it either. I appreciate being seen as something more than my public persona, and people whom work for me know that although I may be demanding, I am also fair. My door is always open, and they feel confident that when they have something to say, I'll be listening.

Someone recently wrote in to ask me how to manage people whom she didn't like. My response was to ask her if she liked anything about any of the people she was attempting to manage. We all have hidden potential, and a good manager will find it. A good manager will also look for what he or she *likes* about the people around them. No one is perfect. We all have strengths and weaknesses. Your attitude toward others plays a big part in surrounding yourself with the right people. If you don't like the people around you, you might start by taking a look at yourself first.

Most of us spend a great deal of our time at our jobs. That fact alone makes it important to carefully assess what kind of people we want to spend it with. What matters to you? What combination of personalities will make the day the most effective for everyone? An organization is ever evolving, as we are, and a good balance is necessary for everyone. Does everyone understand, clearly, what the common goal of the organization is? One reason Don Jr., Ivanka, and Eric have done such remarkable jobs is that they understand—thoroughly—what our goals are and make significant and daily contributions to that end. They work together effectively as a team and individually, which is the ideal representation for any organization.

Make an effort to make your working environment as pleasant and effective as possible. It's not impossible—my organization proves that it's not impossible. Just set the example, and you'll be a magnet for the right people. That's the best way to work with people you like.

Integrity is the essence of everything successful.

—RICHARD BUCKMINSTER FULLER

In Addition to Business: What the Successful Person Needs to Know

I've recently encountered a situation that brought me back to something I had learned a long time ago—that it's not just business acumen but integrity that carries you forward in the business world. It's as simple as keeping your word or, in some cases, remembering what your words were. It seems that for some people, simple isn't always easy.

I came from the world of construction and real estate development, which is known for being demanding and difficult, but it also requires precision. There can't be anything haphazard in construction or people can be injured. "Happenstance" is not acceptable. I've applied that approach to everything I do.

I can remember when a visitor to my offices commented on how many blueprints there were. He said, "Some people have skeletons in their closets, but I can see that Trump has blueprints in his." Sometimes I think people forget that I'm a builder, a developer. That's my core, and blueprints are important. It took me

185

awhile to realize how valuable that background was in forming my discipline as a businessman. It gave me a foundation from which to operate and expand and a tendency toward thoroughness.

There's integrity to building that cannot be compromised. We've all seen the results of hastily constructed buildings in the earthquakes and in other disasters around the world. I will not jeopardize the safety and well-being of people, and if I'm known to be a stickler for details, that is one of the reasons.

Our actions and words will eventually point us toward having a reputation for having integrity or not having integrity. I've been around long enough to know how valuable a commodity candor can be. As a businessperson, it's a strength that can see you through everything.

Another important skill is negotiation. I receive many requests asking me about my negotiation skills, and there's a balance to successful negotiation that many people fail to see. The best negotiation is when both sides win. There's a compromise involved, which means careful listening, and when that is achieved you'll see results that work. Business is an art in itself, and powerful negotiation skills are one of the techniques necessary to facilitate success.

I give a lot of speeches, and one thing I will always emphasize is the importance of passion. If you don't love what you're doing, your margin for success is significantly reduced, and tough times will be much tougher to get through. Passion gives a resiliency that is necessary to achieve great things. Michelangelo is remembered in our time more than any pope or politician of his time simply because he gave the world so much—and against great odds. That guy was intransigent. There is no doubt that he was passionate about what he was doing. When things seem difficult, it's good to remind yourself of someone like that, someone who kept the integrity of his art first and foremost in his mind and actions.

The second point I will bring up when it comes to success is that you cannot give up. You have to keep going and moving forward, no matter what is happening around you or to you. It's a form of positive thinking that is very powerful. A word that comes to mind as a result of this approach is "indomitable." I overcame some great setbacks just by being obstinate. I refused to give in or give up. To me, that's an integrity of purpose that cannot be defeated or interfered with to any significant level. Being steadfast in your intentions can reap great results.

The other word I like to think of along with indomitable is "tenacious." In a way, they are almost interchangeable when it comes to business. Being tenacious will make you indomitable in the long run. The old tortoise versus the hare story still prevails.

With today's globalization, I will emphasize the importance of paying attention to global events. The United States cannot be isolationist. We may be the super power, but what that really means is that we have more responsibility. Our position requires us to be more alert, more careful, and more empathetic than ever. Power is at its best when it's used in the most compassionate way possible.

When it comes to business success, it is equally important to know that success carries the same sort of responsibility. Always know that you can be topped and that you can be toppled over. Keeping that in mind will guarantee that you are in your best form for competition. Even if you are currently the top gun, pretend that you are the underdog. It will improve your insight as well as your vision.

Intrinsic value is a value that has been overlooked in today's marketplace. Everything has a dollar value, and it becomes very black and white. That is necessary in business. We live in a tangible world with tangible needs. But I will say that I often look for the obscure, the gray area that implies a mystery or a value that is more than money alone can carry. I think most people will know what this is—something that is beyond monetary value. I read a story about an art collector who had amassed a fortune in art, but his prized possession was a painting of his deceased son done by a friend of his son's. This painting was hung next to works by Picasso, Matisse, Monet, and Miró. But it mattered most to the art collector. Its intrinsic value far surpassed the millions represented by the masters. When the collector died, he bequeathed his entire collection to the person who bought the painting of his son, which sold for $10.

I mention intrinsic value because as a businessman, it's something that gives integrity and even mystery to everyday business. Not everything is dollars and cents, although in many cases it has to be. Look for the gray areas—it will enhance your life as well as your business sense.

As a businessman, I have realized that "to whom much is given, much is expected." See yourself as having a lot already, and keep your integrity intact. It's the best way to pave your way to a comprehensive success.

Somewhere, something incredible is waiting to be known.

—Carl Sagan

~~~

You Can Be in Charge

That's an empowering thought. It's also a real possibility. If it seems you're being thrown curveballs every day, that means it's time for some strategy. In short, you need to be bigger than your problems are in order to handle what's being delivered.

Here are a few things to think about:

1. What is your creative capital? Many of us have hobbies, knowledge, and experiences that can be turned into something useful in the marketplace. Give this some comprehensive thought. You probably have talents that could be further developed to create a career.

2. Are you lucky? Some people seem to be naturally lucky. Another definition of good luck is the ability to turn bad luck into good luck.

3. Be proactive. Don't be passive or fearful. Just taking the next step can get you to better and even great places. Start today.

4. Be objective and strive to be your own counselor. I listen to others, but I know the final decision is

mine and I hold myself responsible. That in itself is empowering.

5. If you haven't given history enough attention, start doing so today. Also, realize you are in a pivotal time in history, and see it as a challenge as well as an opportunity.

"Creative capital" deserves a bit more explanation. In essence, one way to become rich is to be able to move an idea into your asset column. Those people who've had an innovative idea and put it into production, whether it was for an automobile or for Post-Its, have been able to move their invention from "idea" to "asset" in a very big way.

A lot of great ideas get discarded before they're developed, and some ideas deserve to be discarded before they take up too much time and end up being more of a problem than a solution. This is where objectivity and research are useful.

Let's say you have an idea for a new product or a variation on one that has been successful. The first thing to do is to check out the global marketplace. The best scenario is if you can find a void in that marketplace and find something unique to fill it. It's important to consider that you could have something to offer that would be viable as well as valuable.

In the current economy, many people are being challenged to find alternative venues for income. That can be an exciting time if you approach the situation in a positive light. It's also empowering to think of being an inventor—what doesn't exist yet that could or should exist? That way of thinking will open you up to the possibilities that are definitely there. One important consideration is to make sure you define yourself instead of allowing others to define you. They will limit you when instead you should see that your possibilities are limitless. When it was reported that I was done and in financial ruin in the early 1990s, I took control by refusing to believe that I was finished. That's not the definition I chose for myself, which gave me a resiliency that probably surprised a lot of people.

Another point to consider is that when you allow others to define you, you become a bit of a puppet in their hands. Be very wary of this kind of strategy, because some people need to win by getting their competition out of the way instead of being superior to their competition. Be your own barometer of success. We all experience failures, but that doesn't make us failures, even if others say so. Take control of the circumstance by seeing it in a different light.

Each of us has a different route to our destiny and challenges are part of that path. Keep your self-image strong and intact by defining yourself in the best way possible—every day, no matter what the circumstances might be. Know from the inside out that you have the power to succeed and you will. That's taking control. Your creative capital might be waiting to be discovered.

Most powerful is he who has himself in his own power.

—SENECA

◆

Synergy

Synergy is a word that implies the whole is greater than the sum of its parts. It's a coming together of energies that is made clear by the Greek roots of the word: syn + ergos = *together working*. The word has a scientific application, but it also works for business aptitude—as in, combining forces to create a greater momentum, a greater whole.

This can apply to teamwork as well as to individual enterprise. I may be an entrepreneur, but I also head a large organization, so I know how important this concept is. Teamwork and individual responsibility combine to create a force that will make you far more viable in the marketplace. This is one of the concepts of *The Apprentice* that business students are likely to recognize.

When you have a job, always consider the big picture and the gestalt of the organization first. This is a bit like a negotiation technique—take into consideration where the other side is coming from. How you can contribute to the overall success will be made clearer to you. When everyone works that way, success is much easier to attain. You will also be on the wavelength of the CEO, because it is his or her job to keep the organization healthy, vital, and moving forward.

If you are an entrepreneur, you'll find there are times when you are your own team. I'm surprised sometimes to notice that people can actually be working against themselves. Pay attention to that possibility and cooperate with yourself. Make sure you are airtight by combining the forces within yourself to create a whole. Your efforts will automatically become more effective.

A recent and good example of synergy is my golf course development in Scotland—Trump International Golf Links Scotland, in beautiful Aberdeen. It's been a tremendous but challenging experience due to the complexities of the situation. Everyone got together and we are moving forward, but initially it was my determination to develop this magnificent property that got us going. The synergy was at first individual then it became a significant team effort. It can be a wonderfully effective combination.

DONALD J. TRUMP'S
RECOMMENDED READING

The Art of War
by Sun Tzu
This is a classic book about military strategy written during the sixth century BC.

The Cashflow Quadrant
by Robert Kiyosaki
and Sharon Lechter
This is about working smart and is a good, clear guide to help you move toward financial freedom.

The Power of Positive Thinking
by Norman Vincent Peale
This book was published in 1952 and contains useful concepts to enable successful behavior. I'm a cautious optimist but being optimistic is important to be effective.

The Golden Ratio
by Mario Livio
"The story of phi, the world's most astonishing number." This is fascinating whether or not you are a math whiz.

Team of Rivals: The Political Genius of Abraham Lincoln
by Doris Kearns Goodwin
Goodwin reveals just how brilliant Lincoln was, with a political spin that has historical as well as contemporary interest.

The Last Lion: Winston Spencer Churchill
by William Manchester
This is Manchester's second volume on Churchill. It gives a great insight into Churchill as well as World War II.

No Ordinary Time: Franklin & Eleanor Roosevelt:
The Home Front in World War II
by Doris Kearns Goodwin
This book brings to life a most interesting and pivotal time in U.S. history side by side with the Roosevelts.

Ideas and Opinions
by Albert Einstein
Einstein was not just a scientist, but a great mind at work on many topics, which are covered here.

Essays and Lectures
by Ralph Waldo Emerson
Emerson's writing is lucid and thought provoking, and he provides a balance of thought that can be edifying.

INDEX

197